A Ceremonies Sampler

New Rites, Celebrations, and Observances of Jewish Women

A Ceremonies Sampler

New Rites, Celebrations, and Observances of Jewish Women

Edited by

Elizabeth Resnick Levine

WOMAN'S INSTITUTE FOR CONTINUING JEWISH EDUCATION
San Diego, California

First Printing 1991

Woman's Institute for Continuing Jewish Education
4126 Executive Drive
La Jolla, CA 92037

Library of Congress Card Number: 90-70834
ISBN 0-9608054-9-4

Printed in the United States of America

Contents

Introduction

Jewish women have always lived lives rich with ceremonies. From earliest times in our recorded history, we find rites marking special events in a woman's life cycle. Judges 11:39-40 describes an annual puberty rite in which young girls go out to the hills for four days each year to celebrate their transition to womanhood.[1] Judges 21:20-21 and Ta'anit 4:8 recount elaborate courting rituals. Each year on the fifteenth of Av and on Yom Kippur, Jewish maidens, dressed in white, move in procession from the city to the vineyards to sing and dance with the young men.[2]

Absent from these brief descriptions, however, are the abundance of women's rites and ceremonies that would have taken place within the domestic sphere and private lives of women. These are not recorded in a history that focuses primarily on men and religious cult activities. Leviticus 12:6-8, for example, describes the ritual offering a woman is to bring to the Tent of Meeting following a period of ritual purification after childbirth. Missing from these narratives are concomitant rituals: birthing rites, a weaning ceremony, circumcision feast, and rites led by female specialists, such as midwives.[3] We only can guess what blanks need filling in to have a complete understanding of the ceremonial life of our earliest women.

Now, however, the written record is changing. Not only are learned people gleaning the texts for ceremonies of the past,[4] but also an increasing number of women are taking part in the joy of creating new ceremonies and rituals.

Sometimes we borrow these celebrations from the past and transform them for the present (example: *al-wafaa,* p. 9), but far more often, fresh, original celebrations arise because there is a need for them. This outburst of creativity reflects the health of contemporary Judaism.

This book contains a selected sampling of the innovative ceremonies being developed today. Some of the ceremonies have been shortened in order to include a representative offering of what is being accomplished. The reader will note that twenty years ago we would not have had ceremonies for commitment, women's rabbinic ordination, or hysterectomy, but because our needs are different, so are our ceremonies.

Some of the ceremonies, like the *get* ceremony, are ancillary and are to be used in conjunction with the traditional one so that the woman can surround herself with family, friends, and a liturgy which gives comfort and support. Many of the ceremonies contain prayers with images that the reader may not have been exposed to before, prayers that begin "Let us bless the source of life" (p. 20) or that praise the magnificent Shechinah "Who in wisdom formed women's bodies and created in us unique openings, passageways, organs, and glands" (p. 16).

We hope that the reader will exult with us over these lively yet profoundly-felt works and be inspired to create a ceremony of her own. Other examples, as well as the process for creating ceremonies, can be found in my two-books-in-one, *Midlife, A Rite of Passage, and The Wise Woman, A Celebration* (Woman's Institute for Continuing Jewish Education, 1988) and in Penina V. Adelman's *Miriam's Well: Rituals for Jewish Women Around the Year*, Second Edition (Biblio Press, 1990). Other collections of celebrations can be found in the vast repository at the Jewish Women's Resource Center, a project of the National Council of Jewish

Women, New York Section.

In ancient times, in close-knit communities, it was the responsibility of the elders to help people through rites of passage. In our time, women of all ages are filling this role by creating rituals to reflect contemporary life. They have gone through the initiation process and serve as guides for the rest of us. Now we can journey forth confidently into our Jewish future knowing that there is much to celebrate. These ceremonies show us the way.

Irene Fine, Ph.D.
San Diego, California
January, 1991

---

[1] P. L. Day, ed., *Gender and Difference in Ancient Israel* (Fortress Press: Minneapolis, 1989), 58; C. Meyers, *Discovering Eve: Ancient Israelite Women in Context* (Oxford University Press: New York, 1988), 161.

[2] I. Abrahams, *Jewish Life in the Middle Ages* (Atheneum: New York, 1975), 172.

[3] P. Bird, "The Place of Women in the Israelite Cultus," in *Ancient Israelite Religion,* edited by P. D. Miller, Jr. *et al.* (Fortress Press: Philadelphia, 1987), 409-410.

[4] Among others see, for example, C. Weissler, "The Traditional Piety of Ashkenazic Women," in *Jewish Spirituality from the Sixteenth Century Revival to the Present,* edited by A. Green (Crossroad: New York, 1987), 262-267.

Preparing for Parenthood

Pregnancy and the transition into parenthood are two important life stages which are not adequately celebrated or ritualized in traditional Judaism. During my first pregnancy in 1980, I wanted to acknowledge the holiness of carrying a new life within my body and to explore my own passage into Jewish motherhood. I decided to create a ritual and a special document which would parallel my wedding ceremony and *ketubah* (marriage contract) and mark my transition into the next stage of my family life. Since my husband preferred to focus his attention on writing a creative *brit*-naming ceremony for our child, I planned my ritual for twelve women on the last full moon of my pregnancy.

I thought of my advancing pregnancy as a passage through a constricting tunnel to emergence with a revitalized, fuller identity as a Jewish mother—a birth image. This is also the metaphor of the Exodus from Egypt—*mitzrayim* (Egypt) being a narrow *(tzar)* place of oppression—when the Israelites passed through the (birthing) waters of the Red Sea to accept new ethico-religious obligations at Mt. Sinai. In becoming a mother, I was accepting new responsibilities and a commitment to the future of the Jewish people.

As my women friends gathered at my home on the designated evening, I placed several special objects in the center of our circle: an egg-shaped candle, a rose floating in a bowl of water, cedar incense, a crescent-shaped *challah,* and *kiddush* wine. Each woman added a fruit symbolic of a wish/blessing. We opened the circle by each woman in turn lighting the candle she'd brought, reciting her matrilineage, and passing the flame on to the next woman. This gesture linked us to the chain of Jewish mothers in our personal histories. We recited the *shehecheyanu,* the Hebrew blessing for special occasions that thanks God for bringing us to this joyous moment.

One of my friends led a movement and breathing exercise that took us through the unfolding stages of a blooming bud. With our thoughts focused on birth and growth, we chanted the Hebrew blessings and passed around the wine and *challah*.

The women then spoke about the wishes symbolized in the fruit which each had brought. Each woman's interpretation was unique and original: a kiwi stood for sensitivity, maple syrup for patience, an apple for wisdom, an avocado for fortitude, an orange for courage, and a fig for love. All these qualities were symbolically given to me to empower me in my upcoming motherhood. Then each woman took a colored pencil and filled in a part of the mandala (described below) which I had designed as a representation of my values as a Jewish parent.

Feeling buoyed up by these wishes, I spoke about my hopes and my fears on becoming a mother. Other mothers in the group spontaneously shared their own birthing and mothering experiences. We sang some of my favorite Hebrew songs of inspiration and devotion. One song from Psalm 130 evolved into a chain dance which wove all of us into a cluster of swaying hugs.

The emotional climax of the ceremony for me was the random chanting of personal qualities to empower me to go forth as a "mother in Israel." The love and goodwill directed to me was almost overwhelming, and the memory of it comforted me in my painful labor three weeks later.

The ceremony lasted about one-and-a-half hours and finished with blessing and eating the fruits.

I used my mandala, completed during the ceremony, as a visual focal point to accompany my breathing patterns during natural childbirth. After my daughter's birth, I added her birth data to the design of the mandala and photocopied it onto birth announcements. The framed mandala hangs in my living room as a representation of my goals and values as a parent, just as my egalitarian *ketubah* reflects my views about marriage.

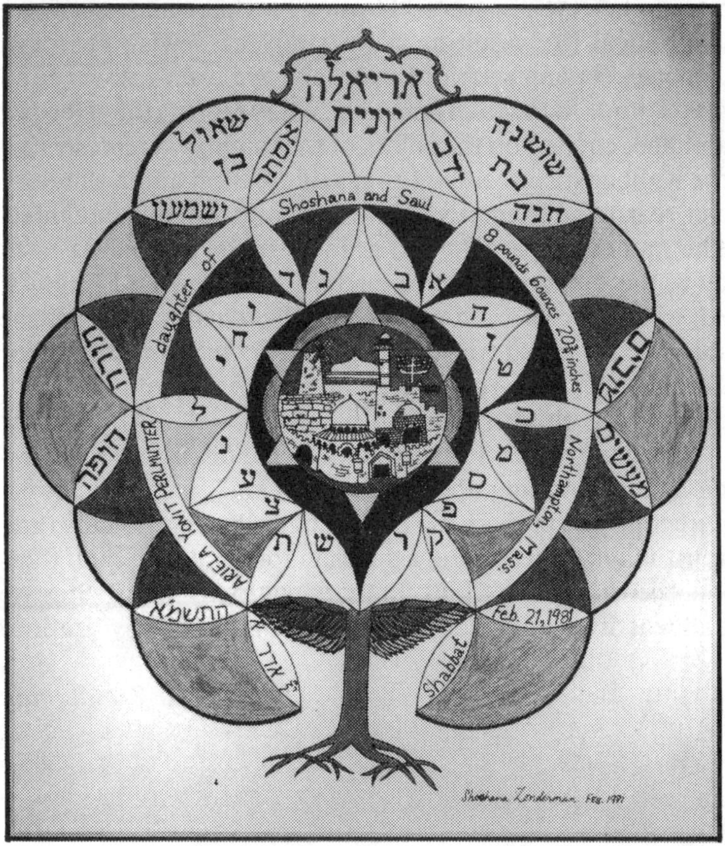

The design of the mandala incorporates concentric circles with Jerusalem on a *magen david* (star of David) at the core. This is a visual link to the *ketubah* which is crowned with a quotation from Psalm 137: "We will elevate Jerusalem to the head of our joy." Jerusalem symbolizes the intense commitment of my husband and myself to the Jewish people, its culture, and its history. Our daughter Ariela's name is like "Ariel," the name used by the prophet Isaiah (29:1) to refer to Jerusalem.

Embedded in one of the circles on the mandala is the traditional Jewish parents' blessing for their children: *Torah* (an ethical life resulting from study of Jewish sources), *chuppah* (loving relationships), and *ma'asim tovim* (good deeds and social activism). The letters of the Hebrew alphabet circling on the colors of the rainbow—representing the Kabbalistic ascending rungs of creation and holiness—can rearrange themselves into blessings for our daughter. The names of parents and grandparents, as well as birth data, are blended into the circles in Hebrew and English. All of the circles are supported by the female symbol in the shape of a winged tree of life (*aitz chayim,* a metaphor for Torah) with deep roots to recall the only lasting gift of a parent to a child: roots and wings.

The weeks which I spent planning and discussing this ceremony and thinking about my values and goals as a Jewish parent helped prepare me psychologically, emotionally, and spiritually for becoming a Jewish mother. More than that, it deepened my conscious commitment to my Jewish lifestyle and reaffirmed my place in our ongoing Jewish civilization.

Shoshana Zonderman

M'ugelet: A Pregnancy Ritual

In 1987 I was pregnant with my first child, Sophia Lilit, and my Jewish women's group, Isha L'Isha, wanted to do a ritual for me. This ritual is adapted from one in Penina Adelman's book, *Miriam's Well.* As I write this, I am about seven months pregnant with my second child and have performed the ritual three more times (with Isha again and two other Jewish women's groups to which I belong)—so I can confirm its efficacy!

I call this ritual *m'ugelet,* which is a Hebrew pun meaning both "she becomes round," referring to the condition of pregnancy, and "she is encircled," the main activity of the ritual.

One of the women in my group brought a long cord which had been wrapped around Rachel's tomb in Israel. In legend, Rachel is often called the mother of Israel, a spiritual presence whose caring for her children continues to this day. Women have made pilgrimages to her tomb for centuries.

The women stood around me in a circle, holding the cord. I recited the following prayer, which is written in the style of Ashkenazi *techinas,* Yiddish women's folk prayers of the 16th through 20th centuries. (My thanks to Dr. Chava Weissler and Rabbi Tracy Klirs whose valuable work on this subject has opened up a vast source of our mothers' religious traditions):

> Merciful and gracious Creator, have compassion on your loving handmaid, __________ bat

> ________, that she may have her child safely and in good health. May the merit of our holy foremothers Sarah, Rivka, Rachel, Leah, Bilha, and Zilpah, and the merit of our great leaders Miriam, Deborah, Hannah, and Judith, sustain me through my time of danger. May You help me avoid unhealthy acts and stay far away from any drink, smoke, or food which might harm the precious life within me. May this child be born in spacious straits, with room to spare. As You opened the Red Sea so that the children of Israel could pass through it unharmed, please open my waters and birth canal so that this child is born safely and without pain. May this little one grow to be a righteous person, always living in the path of Torah and *ma'asim tovim* (good deeds), and may the Jewish people merit true redemption in this one's lifetime. Amen.

I then went to one of the women who was holding an end of the cord. She wrapped the end around my belly and passed me to the woman next to her. As I was passed around the circle of women, the cord encircled my pregnant womb. The women whispered blessings to me such as "good birth!" "healthy baby!" "easy delivery!" etc., forming a symbolic protective space for me and the life I held within me.

Then we sang Jewish feminist composer Faith Rogow's blessing song:

> As we bless the Source of Life
> So we are blessed.
> As we bless the Source of Life
> So we are blessed.
> And the blessing gives us strength,

And makes our visions clear
And the blessing gives us peace
And the courage to dare.
As we bless the Source of Life
So we are blessed.

When I gave birth to Sophie, I took the cord with me to the hospital and held it while I was in labor. Unfortunately, I had to have an emergency C-section. As I lay in the recovery room and regained feeling in the lower part of my body, I found that I was still tightly gripping that cord. Sophie was born whole and healthy, and I made a very quick recovery, easily and comfortably up and about in time for her *brit* ceremony.

Rabbi Jane Litman

References

Adelman, Penina, *Miriam's Well: Rituals for Jewish Women Around the Year.* NY: Biblio Press, 1990, pp. 55, 128.

Klirs, Tracy Guren, "Bizkhus fun sore, Rivke, Rokhl un Leye: The *Tkhine* as the Jewish Woman's Self-Expression." Rabbinical thesis, Hebrew Union College, 1984.

Rogow, Faith, "As We Bless." © 1990 Used with permission.

Weissler, Chava, "The Traditional Piety of Ashkenazic Women," in *Jewish Spirituality from the Sixteenth Century Revival to the Present,* edited by A. Green. NY: Crossroad, 1987, pp. 262-267.

al-wafaa: A Post-Partum Celebration

Bored with baby showers which officially ignore the pregnant woman, six years ago in New York, I twice revived a traditional Yemenite Jewish women's celebration. A post-partum rejoicing, *al-wafaa* celebrates a mother's successful birthing of the baby she has carried for nine months.

Set six weeks apart, both ceremonies were conducted in the home of a woman whose living room was large enough to contain about fifty women. In keeping with tradition, both ceremonies took place in the evening: the first on a weekday and the second on a Sunday.

Although most of the women no longer met regularly *en masse* several times a week, as was customary in Yemen and still is in Israel, I had no trouble getting a dozen women to contribute food and supplies. In fact, the women I contacted responded with considerable enthusiasm.

Like me, most of them had only heard about *al-wafaa*. We were curious to see how the elder females who were born in Yemen, and who had had *al-wafaa,* conducted them.

The room filled up quickly. Women with babies brought them as well. The women's pleasure at being together was evident in the constant talking and laughing. The joyful noise level was raised further by cassette recordings of Yemenite women and men singing women's oral and men's written traditional poem-songs.

Borrowed folding chairs lined the walls. The couch and two deep chairs were reserved for the oldest women. Soda, coffee, and tea went around the room continually. Tables jammed into the tiny dining alcove were hidden by plates of home-baked cakes, *ja'aleh* (the roasted nuts and legumes that must be part of Yemenite Jewish rituals), fruit, and candy. As one plate emptied, another sailed through the kitchen door to replace it.

The center of the floor was rarely empty. Women danced, sat down, or walked away at their pleasure, their places quickly taken by others who had momentarily finished snacking on food and gossip. Cassettes played continually and the talking flowed unabated. Occasionally, one of the older women picked up a borrowed *tarbuqah,* a hand-drum, and accompanied her poem-singing as other women danced.

Conversation criss-crossed the room. . . stories of easy and hard pregnancies and births, the exchanging of significant local news, such as who had just returned from Israel or was leaving New York to visit children and grandchildren in California, and the price of *kabzarah,* the Chinese parsley that is essential to *hilbah* (a dip made from crushed fenugreek seeds and *zahuq,* a combination of crushed hot peppers, garlic, salt, and black pepper). Only a few of the women brought gifts for the mothers.

I danced, ate, sang, took innumerable photographs, listened, and asked questions. In Yemen it was, of course, different.

* * *

In Yemen, on the thirtieth day following delivery, the woman's female relatives and friends gather to applaud the survival of both mother and infant. They pay homage to the miracle of birth which women only are gifted by G–d to perform. They honor the pair's courageous battle with death and acclaim their subsequent rebirth.

Each woman brings food to share with the others and a

gift for the mother. Each sings and dances before the mother and her baby. The women's poem-songs, sung by *maghanniath,* professional women poet-singers, as well as by the less skilled participants, narrate past and imaginary events, as well as feelings women have poeticized regarding conception, parturition, and birth.

Although the celebration is a happy one, the tone is generally muted. In the center of the room, in full view of the participants and around which the women dance, is sometimes placed a tiny wooden coffin, no doubt a reminder that the infant, at least, is not yet out of danger.

al-wafaa comes from the triliteral Arabic root *wf?* from which spring derivations referring to completion, fidelity in fulfilling an obligation, and the imminence of death and redemption. The celebration is a bittersweet one: joyful success flavored with vinegar, the ever-present reality of death's imminence. Perhaps it is that tart-tasting mix that makes the baby shower which has replaced *al-wafaa,* so much more popular.

Dina Dahbany-Miraglia, Ph.D.

Simhat Yoledet: Celebrating the Birth of a Mother

The birth of a child is universally greeted with joy and thanksgiving by family and community. Each culture has its unique ways of welcoming newborn members. In Jewish tradition these include circumcision for boys and naming rituals for boys and girls.

In many traditional communities it is the women's responsibility to provide physical, emotional, spiritual, and intellectual support and nourishment to the new mother—and each time a woman bears a child she is, once again, a new mother. This support comes in many forms:

Physical: taking care of the housework, the cooking, and the other children as mother and baby get to know one another; massaging and feeding mother special foods and drinks to build her strength.

Spiritual: offering prayers, amulets, incense, and isolation to protect the couple during this sensitive and vulnerable time.

Emotional: sharing birth and life stories, anecdotes, and wisdom which let a new mother know that she is not alone in all her range of emotions, responses, and experiences. These stories also provide practical advice for what to do about these emotions and experiences.

Intellectual: It is important for us to remember that our intellectual needs do not end with breast feeding and diaper changes. In fact, these needs and interests are often enhanced and changed by the arrival of children.

Of course, all of these areas overlap and in reality they

cannot be distinguished so neatly one from the other.

The following is a ritual I composed to honor a friend in her third passage to motherhood. It was carried out in Ellen's home with a community of women who gather monthly to celebrate *Rosh Hodesh,* which, according to tradition, is a women's holiday. At this ceremony, Ellen also invited some of her personal friends who were not part of the *Rosh Hodesh* group.

* * *

Participant:

"In Jewish tradition the family and communal lives of women were rarely recorded. We do not know just what kinds of support women offered one another at the time of birth. This evening we will create—or recreate—a celebration for the *yoledet,* the birthing mother—to honor Ellen and Avigail Shifra. Our celebration will incorporate what we know about the needs and desires of birthing women in general and Ellen in particular, and it will include physical, emotional, spiritual, and intellectual nourishment and support. It will also include seven blessings. (In Jewish tradition the number seven symbolizes wholeness.)

"Let us begin as we begin any Jewish celebration—with a cup of wine."

Community:

Baruch Ata Adonai, Eloheinu Melech ha-olam, boray p'ri hagafen.

"Blessed are You, God, Ruler of all, Who creates the fruit of the vine."

Participant:

"In order to help provide for Ellen's physical needs I have asked each of us to bring some freezable, tasty, healthy dish. This will help Ellen in two ways: Not only will it provide food for her family and herself, but also it will allow Ellen to focus her time and energy on other things than cooking in these first weeks of adjusting to being a family of five. The foods are stored in Ellen's freezer, but on the table here are some tasty and healthy foods which we can enjoy now as we continue.

"Even when pregnancy and birth are normal, there is some risk to the health and safety of mother and child. On behalf of Avigail and herself, Ellen will recite *Birkat HaGomel.*"

Ellen:

Baruch Ata Adonai, Eloheinu Melech ha-olam, ha-gomel la-chayavim tovot, sheg'malani kol tuv.

"Blessed are You, God, Ruler of all, Who graciously bestows favor upon the undeserving, even as God has bestowed favor upon me."

Community:

Mi she-g'malech kol tuv, hu yig'malech kol tuv, sela.

"May God Who has blessed you continue to bless you and be with you with all that is good."

Participant:

"As we remember with thanksgiving our safe passage through the risks of childbirth, we also remember that birth is a normal physiological, emotional, and spiritual passage. We thank God for our wondrous bodies."

Community:

Brucha At Shechina, asher yatzra et ha-isha b'chochma, uvar'ah banu nekavim, meyuchadim v'chalulim meyuchadim, gluyim v'yeduim lifnei kiseh kvodech. Im yefateach echad me-hem o yesatem echad me-hem, ee efshar l'hitkayem ulekayem et yeladenu v'yaldatenu. Brucha At Shechina, rof'a kol basar, umafli'a la'asot.

"Blessed are You, Shehina, Who in wisdom formed women's bodies and created in us unique openings, passageways, organs, and glands. These are known and revealed to You. If one of these opens when it should close or closes when it should open, it is impossible for us to live and sustain ourselves or to create and sustain our children.

"Blessed are You, Shehina, Healer of all flesh Who creates and sustains our bodies in wondrous ways."

Community:

Brucha At Shechina, she'astani isha.

"Blessed are You, Shehina, Who has made me a woman."

Participant:

"As we face the daily challenges of balancing family,

community, and career responsibilities, the emotional support we can provide to one another is invaluable. I would like to ask Ellen to share her birth story and/or some other anecdote. Then let us each take a moment to close our eyes and use Ellen's story to guide us in choosing a personal story—words of wisdom and humor—to share with Ellen and each other. We begin with the blessings recited upon hearing good news and the *Shehecheyanu* (thanking God for helping us to reach this milestone in our lives)."

Community:

Baruch Ata Adonai, Eloheinu Melech ha-olam, hatov vehameitiv.

"Blessed are You, God, Ruler of all, Who is good and beneficent."

Community:

Baruch Ata Adonai, Eloheinu Melech ha-olam, shehecheyanu v'kiyyamanu v'higgianu laz'z'man hazeh.

"Blessed are You, God, Ruler of all, Who has brought us to life, sustained us, and brought us to this moment."

Naomi:

"Our intellectual needs continue even though there is less and less time to meet them as the immediate demands of laundry, carpools, meal preparation, story time, bath time, seem to take over our lives. To provide Ellen with some intellectual nourishment, I offer a *dvar Torah* on one of the many birth stories in the Bible to see what our ancestors can teach us about birth, babies, motherhood, children, families."

Community:

Baruch Ata Adonai, Eloheinu Melech ha-olam, asher kidshanu b'mitzvotav v'tzivanu la'asok b'divrei Torah.

"Blessed are You, God, Ruler of all, Whose mitzvot add holiness to our lives and Who gave us the *mitzvah* to study Torah."

Naomi:

"Birth, infancy, motherhood, childrearing are all spiritual experiences, as well as physical and emotional ones. I will pass out some paper and pens and ask each person to write down a personal blessing, prayer, or meditation for Ellen and Avigail, as well as Ron, Leora, and Aryeh. As blessings and prayers should, these will reflect who each of us is, as well as who Ellen is. If we want, we can share these blessings out loud when we are finished. If we prefer, they can remain private. We will put them in this bag (which reminds me of a lawyer's briefcase covered with soft baby-like fabric) for Ellen to keep."

Naomi Bromberg Bar-Yam

Birth Day Celebration

The Background

We both gave birth to our first children one winter. As spring gave way to summer and autumn and another winter, we found ourselves celebrating first birthdays, reaching out to each other for affirmation, eager to hear and speak of what had stayed with us of our birth experiences. We wanted to reexperience the wonder; to explore and celebrate what it meant to be the mother of a one-year-old daughter, then a year later of a two-year-old; in time, what it meant for each of us to be the mother of a son.

This ritual grew from our friendship. We created the ceremony as we came to understand that the birthdays of each of our children signified the birth day of our own selves as mothers, and the profound changes that implied. Many of those changes have intensified our search for ethnic, religious, spiritual, and political self-expression. Throughout the years, we have helped each other look closely at the relationship between our Jewish and feminist values, laughing and crying together when the integration has seemed impossible.

Fed by a joyous appreciation of all we share as Jewish mothers, the ceremony gives form to our evolving sense of what it means and has meant to be the "source of life."

The Ritual

Time: Some time around your child's birthday, preferably a Shabbat.

Setting: A kitchen or other comfortable place to talk.

Celebrants/Participants: From two to a small group of mothers—adoptive, birth, grand-, and co-mothers—who want to remember and sanctify annually their/others' becoming and continuing as mothers.

As the anniversary of each of our children's births comes up each year, we arrange to celebrate *our* "birth" days by finding two hours when we can be alone together. Beginning with a special brunch, we treat ourselves to serious, lively discussion about our experiences as Jewish women who are mothers. Taking this time to concentrate on each other and on ourselves is important.

To evoke the moment we start the ritual with a feminist prayer, such as Marcia Falk's blessings for special occasions, which are rich in mother-birth imagery. We read each prayer aloud, first in Hebrew (as best we can), and then in English:

Kiddush and *Shehecheyanu*

N'varekh et ein ha-chayyim
matzmichat p'ri ha-gafen
v'nishzor et sarigei chayyeinu
b'masoret ha-am.

Let us bless the source of life
that nurtures fruit on the vine
as we weave the branches of our lives
into the tradition.

N'varekh et ma'yan chayyeinu
shehecheyanu v'kiyy'manu v'higgianu
la-z'man ha-zeh.

Let us bless the flow of life
that revives us, sustains us,
and brings us to this time.

As we eat, we share with each other a newly discovered poem by a Jewish woman. This year, a nephew's birth coincided with our birth day ritual. Reminded of our own sons' *brits,* we read Merle Feld's poem, "My Friends Baked Cakes and We Ordered Lox and Whitefish from the Deli" (Wenkart). After responding to the poem, we begin to tell our stories.

One mother begins by prompting the other(s) with questions that go something like these:

> It's (*date*), (*number of*) years since (*child's name*)'s birth. How do you feel at this time of year? What do you find yourself thinking about? The birth? The child as s/he is now? What would you like to tell me about the birth story? When you think back on this year of mothering, what do you remember most?

We have found that talking to a devoted listener about any and all of these questions fulfills important needs for self-celebration, at a time when we otherwise focus entirely on our child, neglecting to mark our own significant moment.

Whenever appropriate, the listening friend comments on something wonderful that she has heard or knows about this woman as mother/nurturer, noting the importance of nurturing in the world. She might praise her by naming a particular nurturing act. Or she may ask: "What has helped you to give your most loving self to the people you live with, work with, spend time with?"

Then we focus on the birth experience again, this time connecting our celebration of the mothering self—thoughts about our own life-giving, life-sustaining capacity—with thoughts about God and our Jewish identity. Since we're both on spiritual journeys in search of meaningful ways of being Jewish and feminist, having struggled for years with the meaning of God in our lives, this next question provides an annual opportunity to talk about a difficult, elusive subject. One of us asks the celebrant: "Thinking about ________________'s birth, thinking about your feminist spiritual journey as a Jewish woman, what does God mean to you this year?"

We end the discussion part of our ritual here; hugs, sighs, and tears naturally express our gratitude for this occasion. To conclude, we want something that will help us retain the feelings we have allowed to surface: intense feelings about each other, our children, our mothers, our grandmothers, ourselves, and the world. We sing together Faith Rogow's beautiful "As We Bless," which we learned a few years ago at a Shabbat service organized by the Jewish Women's Caucus of the National Women's Studies Association. We sing it over and over—aloud when we're together, and later silently, as we continue our living, weaving, struggling—blessed by a vision of women's strength, peace, and courage.

As we bless the Source of Life
So we are blessed.
As we bless the Source of Life
So we are blessed.

And the blessing gives us strength,
And makes our visions clear
And the blessing gives us peace
And the courage to dare.
As we bless the Source of Life
So we are blessed.

Jerilyn Fisher and Wendy Goulston

References

"Kiddush" and "Sheheheyanu" are excerpted from *The Book of Blessings* by Marcia Falk. Copyright © 1990 by Marcia Lee Falk. Forthcoming from HarperCollins Publishers, Inc. Reprinted by permission.

Rogow, Faith, "As We Bless." © 1990 Used with permission.

Wenkart, Henny, ed., *Sarah's Daughters Sing*. Hoboken, NJ: KTAV Publications, 1990.

B'rit B'not Yisrael: Welcoming a Daughter Into the Covenant

If women are to be full participants within Jewish life, full partners of the covenant and not marginal Jews who stand on the periphery of privilege and responsibility, there must be a ceremony (more than a naming) which marks a girl's entrance into the *covenant* of the Jewish people, which views her as heir to her people's heritage, potential witness to God, and contributor to community. The first version of this ceremony appeared in the early 1970's. The voices of mothers and fathers, the experiences of facilitating the ceremony have helped to change and fashion the ritual over the last two decades. Yet it still remains fluid. New voices will continue to shape its growth.

The Rabbi opens with words of welcome and blessing.

During the ceremony the mother and father are encircled by a community of men and women, relatives and friends, who symbolically represent the covenant community into which the child is welcomed. After the child is brought into the room, traditional words of welcome are recited.

B'rucha haba-a b'shem Adonai.

Blessed are you who bear the divine presence.

Then the mother holds the child and says:

> My daughter, my child, you have been as dear to me as my own breath. May I hold you gently now with the love to keep you close and with the strength to let you grow.

She hands the child to the father:

> My daughter, my child, a piece of my life is you. You have grown to life apart from me, but now I hold you close to my heart and cradle you in my arms with my love.

The parents then recite together:

> We have been blessed with the gift of new life. We have shared love and pain and joy in bringing our daughter into life and have been privileged to participate in the marvel and beauty of creation.
>
> By the way in which we live, we aspire to teach our daughter to become a caring and loving person. We hope that in seeking to fulfill herself, she will also accept her responsibilities to others and to her heritage. We dedicate ourselves to the creation of a Jewish home and to a life of compassion for others, hoping that our daughter will grow to cherish and emulate these ideals.
>
> God of all generations, bless our daughter and bless us with the gift of health so we may grow together loving Torah, pursuing justice, seeking Shalom.

Baruch Ata, Adonai, M'kor ha-chayim, m'sameach hahorim im yaldayhem.

Blessed is the holy source of life who causes parents to rejoice with their children.

Rabbi:

In Jewish folklore Elijah is regarded as a forerunner of the Messianic Age, the one who announces the "advent of the Messiah." As we recall Elijah at this ceremony, we rekindle our faith that every human life may yet bring about *y'mot hamashiach,* the era of harmony and peace for all people.

(The infant is held by the Sandek.)

Zeh hakisei shel Eliyahu...

This is the chair of Elijah. May his memory be for a blessing. Rejoicing with the birth of new life, we look forward to a future of human fulfillment. Bestow abundant peace upon those devoted to Torah and grant them strength to carry forth its teachings. Happy are we who approach this sacred moment, who are brought here to the dwelling of God.

Parents:

Baruch ata Adonai eloheinu melech ha-olam asher kidshanu b'mitzvotav v'tzivanu l'hachnis et biteinu b'vrit am Yisrael.

Blessed by the presence whose sanctity fills our lives, we bring our daughter into the covenant of the people of Israel.

In the presence of this circle of loved ones and friends, we give to our daughter the name ______________, in Hebrew ______________ bat ______________ v'______________.

We have chosen to name our daughter after ______________. May she grow to ______________
______________________________________.

May ______________ become a name respected and honored for wisdom and good deeds—Torah and *Ma'asim Tovim*.

As parents we commit ourselves to be her models and guides. May God's blessings rest upon our daughter now and always.

The next section (in box) uses the Shabbat as a symbol of the covenant. The ceremony may be performed at other times by deleting these paragraphs.

Parents:

Blessed by the presence whose sanctity fills our lives, we faithfully remember the covenant and are true to its promise. Our God and God of our mothers, God of Sarah, Rebecca, Rachel, and Leah, accept and strengthen us on this Sabbath Day.

Throughout the generations, the Shabbat has been a sign of covenantal commitment and Messianic hope which has inspired generations of our people with the drive to creativity and the values of human dignity. Therefore on this Shabbat (*name of Shabbat*), we bring our daughter into the covenant of the people of Israel.

Rabbi:

V'shamru v'nei Yisrael et ha-Shabbat la'asot et ha-Shabbat l'dorotam brit olam beini u'vein b'nai Yisrael ot hi l'olam ki sheyshet yamim asa Adonai et ha-shamayim v'et ha-aretz u'vayom ha'shiviyi Shabbat v'yinafash.

The descendants of Israel shall keep Shabbat, making Shabbat throughout all their generations, an everlasting covenant. Between me and Israel's descendants shall it be a sign eternally. For in six days God made skies and earth, and on the seventh day God ceased and drew a breath of rest.

Rabbi:

Mi shebeirach Sarah, Rivka, Rachel v'Leah u'Miryam han'vi-ah, v'Avigayil, v'Ester ha-malchah bat Avichayil, hu y'vareich et ha-yaldah ha-n'ima hazot. V'yikarei sh'ma b'yisrael ____________ bat ____________ v'____________ b'mazal tov uvish'at b'rachah. Vizchu avi-ah v'ima l'gadla b'vriut uv'shalom um'nucha l'Torah l'chuppah ul'maasim tovim. Hodu la'Adonai ki tov ki l'olam chasdo. Zot hak'tana ____________ g'dolah tihiye. *

May God who blessed Sarah and Rebecca, Rachel and Leah, Miriam, the prophetess, Avigail, and Esther, the Queen, bless this beloved child, and let her name be known in Israel as ____________ bat ____________ v'____________.

May her name be known for good and for blessing. May her mother and father be privileged to see her grow in health, peace, and contentment.

Give thanks to God for what is good, for covenant love that endures forever.

May this little child, ____________, grow into womanhood as a blessing to her family, the Jewish people, and humanity. As she has entered the covenant of our people, so may she grow into a life of Torah, *huppah,* and good deeds.

---

* Adapted from Seder Zeved HaBat (Sephardic naming ritual for girls).

All present:

K'sheym shenikn'sah labrit kein tikaneis l'torah, ul'chuppah ul'maasim tovim.

As she has been brought into the covenant of our people, so may she attain the blessings of Torah, *huppah,* and good deeds.

Parents may invite all children present to gather around the newborn. Parents say: "You are our tomorrow—a new generation. Your new friends welcome you."

Children respond: *"Heveynu Shalom Alayich."*

Parents:

As we celebrate the birth of our child, we pledge ourselves to help make a world in which all children can live in safety and in peace. "All your children shall be taught of God and great shall be the peace of your children" (Isaiah 54:13).

(Siblings may pass out something sweet to the other children.)

Parents lift a glass of wine and say:

Baruch Ata Adonai, Eloheinu Melech ha-olam, borei p'ri hagafen.

Blessed is the presence whose sanctity fills our

lives and ripens fruit on the vine.

Parents drink the wine. As one parent gives a taste of wine to the child, the other recites:

My dove, in the clefts of the rock
In the shelter of the cliff
Let me see your face.
Let me hear your voice.
For your voice is sweet
And your face, beautiful.
(Song of Songs 2:14)

Rabbi:

Y'var'chech Adonai v'yishm'rech
Yaer Adonai panav elaiyich vechuneich
Yisa Adonai panav elaiyich v'yasem lach shalom.

May God bless you and keep you.
May God be with you and be gracious unto you.
May God show you kindness and give you peace.

Parents:

Baruch Ata Adonai, Eloheinu Melech ha-olam, shehecheyanu v'kiyimanu v'higianu lazman hazeh.

Blessed by the presence whose sanctity fills our

lives, we give thanks for life, health, and this sacred moment.

Rabbi Sandy Eisenberg Sasso

To my husband, Rabbi Dennis C. Sasso, whose linguistic, liturgical, and editorial skills helped to create this ritual, I owe my deepest appreciation and love.

(Some of these prayers were first printed in the *Reconstructionist,* and the *"B'rit B'not Yisrael"* is being prepared for the forthcoming *Reconstructionist Rabbi's Manual.*)

Naming Ceremony for a Daughter

We wanted to create a ceremony to welcome our new daughter to the world and to the covenant of the Jewish people, in much the same way that we had welcomed our son two years earlier at his *bris*. Friends and family gathered at our home on the evening of the first new moon after Molly's birth. The ceremony began with music. A friend performed a violin solo which she had composed especially for the occasion.

Molly's Mother: In Jewish ritual the celebration of Rosh Hodesh — the Festival of the New Moon — is seen as symbolic of the Shekhinah, the feminine aspect of God. For this reason we chose to link the blessing of the New Moon with the naming of our daughter in this ceremony which welcomes her to the covenant of the people of Israel. We hold this ceremony outside so that we can see the New Moon.

Molly's Father: When Israel was to receive the Torah, God said to them: I am giving you the Torah. Present good guarantors to me, and I shall give it to you. They said: Let our ancestors be our guarantors. God said: Your ancestors are not sufficient guarantors. They said: Our prophets can be our guarantors. God said: The prophets are not sufficient guarantors. They said: Let our children be our guarantors. And God said: They are certainly good guarantors. For their sakes, I will give the Torah to you.

Kiddush for the New Moon — Rabbi Laura Geller

Kiddush for Wine — Molly's Maternal Grandfather

Naming Blessing — Rabbi Geller: Our God and God of those who have gone before us, preserve this child to her mother and father, and let her name be called in Israel: Mirit Batya bat Daveed Yeeshai v' Esther.

Blessing of the Covenant — Molly's Parents: You abound in blessings, Adonai, ruling over time and space, who has made us holy through Your commandments and commanded us to bring our daughter into the covenant of Abraham and Sarah, the parents of the people of Israel.

All Respond: As she has entered into the covenant, so may she enter into Torah, *chuppa,* and a life of good deeds.

Drinking of Wine

Molly's Parents: This is the same wine cup that we drank from at our wedding and the same wine cup that we drank from at Jesse Max's *bris*. Today, as you, Molly Bess, drink from this same cup, we say to you: Though we could not have imagined you, you are who we wanted, who we prayed for. Now that you are with us, we promise to love and to care for you and to let you become the person you choose to become. We hope that person is one who cherishes friends and family; who believes in herself, even when others may doubt her; and who leads a life that helps to make this a better world.

Sh'hechianu — Molly's Paternal Grandfather

Parents Read Letter to Molly Bess:

Dear Molly Bess:

You are named Molly in honor and in loving memory of your mother's Great-aunt Mollie, sister of my grandfather. I remember her as a delicate and beautiful woman, artistic and creative. I still use a small crocheted sewing kit Great-aunt Mollie made when I was a little girl. Someday it will belong to you.

You are named Bess in honor and in loving memory of your mother's Great-aunt Bess, sister of my grandmother. Great-aunt Bess took care of me when I was growing up. I remember her laughter, her tears, her gentleness, her love, and her kindness. She loved me and would have loved to know you.

May the qualities and inner beauty of these women shine in you. Mollie was also your father's grandmother's name. She taught her children to be spiritual and generous people and to treasure family, Torah, and *mitzvot.* We hope you will carry on this tradition.

You are the daughter we wanted. You give us balance. You complete us. We have for you the same wish that we had for your brother: That you have a long and healthy life, and we hope one day you have a child of your own so that you may know how much we love you.

Mom and Dad

Paternal Grandmother: May You who blessed our fathers and our mothers bless this child and keep her from all harm. Grant, O God, that she seek peace and pursue justice in the world. May she spread light to all who know her. May her heart be wide open to your Holy Torah, that she may study and teach, faithfully observe and courageously act.

Maternal Grandmother: Martin Buber wrote, "Every person born into this world represents something new, something that never existed before, something original and unique. Every single person is a new thing in the world and is called upon to fulfill her particularity in the world."

All Sing: *Siman Tov u'Mazal Tov u'Yehey Lanu u'Lchol Yisrael.*

A buffet supper followed the ceremony.

Ellen Sandler and Dennis Danziger

Weaning Ceremony

Maria:

Before we begin our Seder, we will have a short ceremony to commemorate the weaning of our daughter, Artemis. We will combine this ceremony with Havdalah, the traditional service at the end of the Sabbath. Havdalah means separation. We celebrate the separation of Shabbat from the rest of the week, and we also celebrate Artemis' weaning as a separation from me.

We note that Havdalah does not mourn the passing of sacred time, but rather that it celebrates the fact of difference, of entering upon another phase of life's cycles. We take note of our differences around this table and look upon them as a source for celebration as well.

Our idea for a weaning ceremony, as well as some specific passages, comes from Rabbi Laura Geller, who devised such a ceremony for her son's weaning. Weaning, separation, has happened before. We were once one body. It will happen again, many times in our lives. Our hope is that we learn to allow Artemis to grow in her own way, to see her as a separate being, but always feeling the same love we have had for her.

Harry:

Then Sarah said, "God has brought me laughter; everyone who hears will laugh with me." And she added,

"Who would have said to Abraham
That Sarah would suckle children!
Yet I have borne a son in his old age."

The child grew up and was weaned, and Abraham held a great feast on the day Isaac was weaned.

(Genesis 21:6-8)

Today we present to Artemis her own kiddush cup, to symbolize her increasing ability to drink from other sources. Artemis was weaned at her eighteenth month. Eighteen is a symbol for life, *chai,* as in the toast *"l'Chaim,"* "to Life." At this time we recite the traditional blessing for reaching a joyous time, the *"Shehecheyanu,"* given below in both its masculine and feminine forms:

Baruch ata Adonai, Elohaynu Melech ha'olam, shehecheyanu, v'kiy'manu, v'higiyanu lazman hazeh.

Brucha Yah Shechinah, Elohaynu Malkat ha'olam, Shehecheeatnu, v'keeyamatnu, v'hee-geeatnu lazman hazeh.

Blessed are You, Ruler of the Universe, who has given us life, sustained us, and enabled us to reach this season.

(Together we read "On Children" from Kahlil Gibran's *The Prophet* and listen to the musical version recorded by Sweet Honey in the Rock.)

Maria:

A Rabbinic Commentary (Midrash):

> He drew out for me because he delighted in me. (Psalm 18:20) Rabbi Yochanan explained the verse as follows: God drew out her breast to give me Torah.

Tonight we start our feast with the blessing over wine, using white wine to symbolize mother's milk.

Kiddush:

> *Baruch ata Adonai, Elohaynu Melech ha'olam, borei p'ri hagafen.*
>
> *Brucha Yah Shechinah. Elohaynu Malkat ha'olam, borayt p'ri hagafen.*
>
> Blessed are You, Ruler of the Universe, Creator of the fruit of the vine.

All:

Enough for me to keep my soul tranquil and quiet
like a child in its mother's arms,
as content as a child that has been weaned.
(Psalm 131:2)

* * * * *

We continue with our Havdalah and Seder service.

Maria Papacostaki and Harry Brod

Personal Prayers

There are many moments during pregnancy and birth which call for a prayerful response. Our tradition is too often silent when the need for ritual expression is great. The following are some attempts to give form to the yearning of our souls.

On Learning of a Pregnancy

Together:

We stand breathless before the Power of Creation that works through us to bring forth new life. We tremble with fear and with joy.

Woman:

Deep inside me a seed is growing. I am afraid, and I am filled with ecstasy.

Together:

May this promise of life come to be—our child. We trust in the source of life, this power which grips us within and yet transcends us. Protect this fragile new beginning. May we find love and strength to nurture this gift of fertility and life. Sheltered under wings of love, may we grow to be partners with the source of life in the miracle of creation.

Baruch Ata Adonai, Eloheinu Melech ha-olam, shehecheyanu v'kiyamanu v'higianu lazman hazeh.

Blessed by the presence whose sanctity fills our lives, we give thanks for life, health, and this sacred moment.

On the Birth of a Child

How wonderful is this moment as we stand at the edge of the mystery of life. Our daughter/son, how small and beautiful you are. You grasp our fingers, and we hold you close. Let our arms be your love cradle; our whispered prayer, your lullaby song. You are little lower than an angel, touched by glory, crowned with splendor.

In awe and gratitude for this precious gift of life, we celebrate our partnership in the miracle and beauty of creation. Our hearts overflow with joy, and we utter words of blessing.

Baruch Ata Adonai, Eloheinu Melech ha-olam oseh ma-aseh b'resheet.

God of the generations, God of new beginnings, this is Your promise of tomorrow, Your image, a reflection of Your divine love. Teach us to be mother and father, worthy of this sacred trust of new life. Sustain us and our daughter/son in health and in love. We are thankful for the beauty of our lives together, which in a tender and powerful love has brought a new life into the world.

Baruch Ata Adonai, Eloheinu Melech ha-olam, shehecheyanu v'kiyyamanu v'higgianu laz'z'man hazeh.

Blessed by the presence whose sanctity fills our lives, we give thanks for life, health, and this sacred moment.

On Bringing a Child Home for the First Time

With joy and anticipation we bring our son/daughter into our home for the first time.

Ma tovu ohalecha, Yaacov, mish'k'notecha, Yisrael.

How lovely are your tents, O Jacob, your dwelling places, O Israel.

May our home always be a *mikdash ma'at,* a small sanctuary, filled with your presence.

May our home be your sanctuary—our child—a place where arms shall cradle you and voices sing you lullabies, where hands shall uphold you and eyes delight to watch you grow.

In this home may we reach out to each other in love.

In this home may our hearts and those of our children be turned to one another.

In this home may we create bonds of trust and care that will keep us close as we grow together as a family.

Barchaynu Avinu kulanu k'echad b'or panecha.

Bless us, source of Life, all of us together with the light of Your presence.

On Adoption of a Child

We have been blessed with the precious gift of a child. After so much waiting and wishing, we are filled with wonder and with gratitude as we call you our daughter/son. Our son/daughter, our child, you have grown to life apart from us, but now we hold you close to our hearts and cradle you in our arms with our love. We welcome you into the circle of our family and embrace you with the beauty of a rich tradition.

We pledge ourselves to the creation of a Jewish home and to a life of compassion for others, hoping that you will grow to cherish and emulate these ideals.

God of new beginnings, teach us to be mother and father, worthy of this sacred trust of life. May our daughter/son grow in health, strong in mind and kind in heart, a lover of Torah, a seeker of peace. Bless all of us together within your shelter of Shalom.

Rabbi Sandy Eisenberg Sasso

Seder Kabbalat Ahkaroot: Accepting the Loss of the Dream for a Biological Child

Introduction

We created this ceremony to help us mourn and accept our inability to conceive a biological child, to share our disappointment with friends and family, and to enable us to move ahead with our lives after infertility.[1] We have drawn from Jewish sources that deal with themes related to barrenness, death, bondage, freedom, and transitions. We hope to counter the insensitivity found in traditional Jewish interpretations of childlessness as a test of faith, divine punishment, or grounds for a husband to divorce his wife.[2] Individuals and couples who share our fate should try to personalize this service by telling about their own experiences and selecting materials which are meaningful to them. Creating the service together proved to be as healing to us as conducting it before a group of our friends and relatives.

Naming of the Ceremony

Seder means "the order (of the service)." Though *Kabbalat* usually refers to the "welcoming" of Shabbat, it also connotes accepting, crying out against, and consoling. *Ahkaroot* means infertility or barrenness. Thus, *Seder Kabbalat Ahkaroot* signifies the order of rituals for crying out against, consoling ourselves about, and ultimately accepting the loss of our dream to have a biological child.

Opening of Ceremony and *Tashlich*

With meditative music in the background, the guests read an explanation of why we chose to create the service. Then they listened to a part of Bonnie Raitt's song, "Nick of Time," which deals with delayed parenthood and the aging process.[3] The first reading was the passage about Hannah's infertility from 1 Samuel 1:1-10 which ends with: "And she was in bitterness of soul and prayed to the Lord and wept in anguish."

We jointly responded:

> We, too, have wept and felt the anguish of Elkanah and Hannah, Abraham and Sarah, Isaac and Rebecca, and Jacob and Rachel, the moment they feared they might never have children. We are haunted by the cry of Rachel to Jacob: "Give me children or I shall die" (Genesis 30:1).

We spoke of the emotional pain caused by infertility. We noted how in modern times faith in medical miracles has replaced faith in God as a cure for infertility, but added that dependence on high-tech procedures can become an obsession, which we illustrated with a poem about contemplating continuing infertility treatment after too many failures.[4]

After everyone read from Ecclesiastes 3:5, ending with the line, "A time to embrace, and a time to refrain from embracing," we jointly declared:

> Our time to plant has ended; our time to mourn has begun; we must weep before we can laugh.

> In the recesses of our minds, however, there still lingers a thought that it might have worked the next time. Therefore, we need to cast away our regrets and "what ifs" into the ocean like the symbolic sins we throw into the water on *Rosh Hashanah* to begin the year with a clean slate. To paraphrase the Prophet Micah, "God will have compassion on us. We will cast all our qualms and dim hopes into the depths of the sea" (Micah 6:19).

We crumbled some bread in our hands and threw it into the water.

The Memorial Service

We mourned the death of our dream by performing a *Keriah* ritual, but instead of cutting a black ribbon, we cut and wore blue and pink ribbons because we will never know what the gender of our baby would have been. Next we read a prayer originally written to memorialize a miscarriage:

> May the One who shares sorrow with Your creation be with us now as we experience the loss of potential life. We are sad as we think of our hopes for this unborn one, as in our minds we imagine what might have been.
>
> Life is a fabric of different emotions and experiences. Now, while we experience life's bitterness and pain, be with us and sustain us. Help us to gather strength from within ourselves, from each other, and from our friends.
>
> Blessed Are You, O Divine Presence, Who shares sorrow with Your Creation.[5]

Following this, everyone joined us in the recitation of the *Kaddish* in both Hebrew and English.

The Seder of Condolence

We explained the traditional significance of the following foods eaten at the *Shiva* meal after a funeral, the *Passover Seder,* and *Rosh Hashanah:* hard-boiled eggs symbolizing the life cycle, bread symbolizing the staff of life, salt-water symbolizing the tears of our despair, horseradish symbolizing the bitterness of failure, honey symbolizing the sweetness of liberation from infertility, and wine symbolizing joy.

We listed the ten plagues of our infertility, taking a drop of wine out of the cup for each one: denial, anger, shame, marital stress, isolation from and envy of friends who have biological children, reproductive regimentation, uncompensated medical costs, depression, loss of control, and death of the dream of the first born.

We dipped the egg into the water and ate it to remember the tears we shed over the two miscarriages we experienced. We made and ate a sandwich of horseradish, honey, and bread to signify how a bitter ending may precede a sweet beginning and that happiness and sadness are part of human existence. Everyone said the traditional blessings over *maror* and bread.

We ended the *Seder* with a responsive reading of a new *Rosh Hashanah* prayer about the qualities we hope God will help us develop in response to various life crises. For example, "If we must face sorrow, help us to learn sympathy."[6]

Shehecheyanu* and *Havdalah

Everyone recited the *Shehecheyanu,* which thanks God "for sustaining us, and for enabling us to reach this season."

We explained that our *Havdalah* separates the dark years

of our infertility from the upcoming lighter years when we will either adopt or choose to be childfree. We read a passage about no longer considering ourselves infertile because from now on, we would define our lives according to what we *do* and *can* have, rather than according to what we *don't* have.[7]

We performed the *Havdalah* service, lighting the double-braided candle and declaring:

> We must distinguish between the heartbreak of infertility and the joy of transcending it. We must separate our pain and grief from the new generative opportunities that lie ahead of us.

We raised the cup of wine and everyone said the blessing over it. We held up the spice-box and smelled the spices to invigorate the new spirit we now possess as we look to the future. Then everyone sniffed it and said the blessing over it. Everyone recited the blessing over fire and the final *Havdalah* blessing as the candle was extinguished in a full cup of wine that overflowed like the full life we hope to lead.

Conclusion of Ceremony

We confessed that our struggle with infertility initially had strained, but subsequently had strengthened our marriage. In this regard, we read a *midrash* which tells the story of a man who planned to divorce his childless wife. His rabbi commanded him to throw a party to celebrate the divorce. At the party, the man told his wife to keep whatever item in his house was most precious to her. After he drank too much wine and fell asleep, his wife ordered her servants to carry him to her father's house. When he awoke, she told him that he was the most precious thing to her. Moved by her love, he remained married to her.[8]

We related how people always ask whether we have a family. We now reply by telling them, "Yes, we have each other! If we have learned anything from this ordeal, it is that love is far greater than reproduction." We removed the *Keriah* ribbons and replaced them with red rose corsages. Then we played Debbie Friedman's, "Arise My Love," whose lyrics are from the Song of Songs 2:10-13.[9] The guests shared relevant readings or their own personal thoughts after the service.

Bonnie and Lawrence Baron

---

[1] Gay Becker, *Healing the Infertile Family: Strengthening Your Relationship in the Search for Parenthood* (Bantam Books, New York, 1990), pp. 138-156.

[2] Michael Gold, *And Hannah Wept: Infertility, Adoption, and the Jewish Couple* (Jewish Publication Society: Philadelphia, 1988), pp. 17-53.

[3] Bonnie Raitt, "Nick of Time," *Nick of Time* (Capitol Records: Hollywood, 1989).

[4] Margaret Rampton Munk, "Mother's Day," in *Without Child: Experiencing and Resolving Infertility,* Eds. Ellen Sarasohn Glazer and Susan Lewis Cooper (Lexington Books, Lexington, 1988), pp. 162-163. Other books which are good sources for readings for this service are: Mary Martin Mason, *The Miracle Seekers: An Anthology of Infertility* (Perspectives Press: Fort Wayne, 1987) and Kassie

Schwan, *The Infertility Maze: Finding Your Way to the Right Help and the Right Answers* (Contemporary Books: Chicago and New York, 1988).

[5] This prayer, written by Rebecca T. Alpert, originally appeared in *The Reconstructionist,* Vol. 51, Issue 1, Sept. 1985, p. 4. She has given her permission for its re-publication here.

[6] "To Face the Future," from *A Tapestry of Prayer* (Congregation Beth Am: Solana Beach, CA).

[7] Jean W. Carter and Michael Carter, *Sweet Grapes: How to Stop Being Infertile and Start Living Again* (Perspectives Press: Indianapolis, 1989), pp. 14-15.

[8] Song of Songs Rabbah 1:4 as cited in Gold, pp. 46-47.

[9] Debbie Friedman, "Arise My Love," *Ani Ma-amin* (Sing Unto God: undated, Houston).

Midlife Covenant:
Healing Ritual after Hysterectomy

I prepared a ritual to help me resolve my grief around the loss of my womb through hysterectomy. It is a ceremony designed to help support my transition into the next fruitful stage of life. My surgery took place on April 27, 1989. The ceremony followed and helped complete my physical and emotional healing. It took place on the summer Solstice.

For me, the sun reference represented the element of fire, the eternal light, and the heated passion which goes along with my public commitment to live the concept of *tikkun,* to heal, repair, and transform the world. This involved placing before women new ways of repairing the feminine in ourselves, our men, our culture.

Even though I considered celebrating this ritual on Rosh Hodesh, the more traditional time for a women's ceremony because of its connection to the new moon, it was the sun that I saw in my imagination. I understood that some reference to the moon and life cycle was appropriate and should be incorporated into the liturgy. The choice of the day, however, needed to represent both a release from my monthly biological cycle and a transition from the lunar state of reflected light to a more heightened sense of the need to generate my own creative direction.

My womb, which I had retained from surgery (this required careful and consistent collaboration with both the surgeon and hospital pathologist), was returned to the earth in a greenware pottery vessel of my own making. This, to allow for rapid reabsorption into dust by the earth.

A *minyan* of women was called together by blowing the shofar. The *minyan* consisted of women important to my life and representing all phases of the life cycle. The guests gathered in the house where the fathers and children organized the potluck dinner. My youngest daughter, Anna, played the *niggun* I had written for my bat mitzvah on her violin, a signal for the women to follow me to the garden. The ceremony was held at 7:00 p.m. to represent the seven days of creation.

Nancy blows shofar and says:

The sound of the shofar proclaims renewal of the world, for the New Year, and for the Jewish people. I have blown the shofar today to gather us together. It represents personal renewal, as well as renewal in the faith for Jewish women. As our own experience of the life force emerges, may we integrate it within ourselves and connect it to traditional liturgy.

This is a prayer I sang as a young girl on the pulpit of our synagogue:

> May the words of my mouth,
> and the meditations of my heart,
> Be acceptable
> Before thee O Lord,
> My rock and my redeemer, Amen.

Let's sit in a circle quietly, eyes closed, hands joined. This completes the life cycle circle and facilitates a sense of connection to each other and to the life force, as we experience it. (I then shared a poem I wrote in fear and grief before deciding for my surgery.)

Let us bow our heads and sit a brief, symbolic *shiva*. Though no death has occurred, it will help me feel your support and acknowledgment of the loss of my womb, as well as the reality of my grief. (I read aloud Drorah Setel's "Blessing for the New Moon," from *Miriam's Well: Rituals for Jewish Women Around the Year,* by Penina V. Adelman, Biblio Press, Fresh Meadows, NY [1986], page 22.)

This marks the symbolic resolution of my grief over the loss of the organic center of my fertility and the place that my lovely daughters began their lives. I am grateful for your affirmation and comfort.

Together:

(All stand) Recite the *Shehecheyanu.*

Nancy moves to center of the circle

All:

> Arise, shine, for your light has come and the glory
> of the Shekhinah will shine within you.
> (paraphrase of Isaiah 60:1)

Nancy:

This is a moment for each of you to offer your own blessing to me in the assembled *minyan.* I would like you to accept my blessing in return. As Martin Buber has pointed out: We can meet God with a genuine dialogue with others. I would like to mention women not present who have yet unresolved grief in relation to their hysterectomies and a prayer that they find comfort and completion around this event. I present a daisy, with a sun-like center, in appreciation to my friends. (I then read a poem I had written after the surgery in thanks to Her.)

Two holes, about a foot deep, have been dug in the garden before the ceremony. I stand between them holding my womb in a hard pottery bowl to have it blessed and purified by the pouring of water from a pottery pitcher. I now join both parts of my life together by the planting of my womb. We draw from our depths the essentials of our sustenance. Our spiritual thirst has caused us to look for new ways of cleansing our bodies and souls.

All say: (While a friend pours water over the womb)

> Women are like water.
> We flow and flow and flow.
> Shechinah is like water.
> She bubbles from below.

Nancy: (Transfers womb to greenware bowl for planting.)

I offer my womb as a covenant, returning it to the earth, honoring the Source of all life. As I plant it in the ground, my mourning is complete and I am released from this part of my life. (We planted two pear tree saplings, one over the womb and the other in the empty hole.)

Sara:

I cover this gift with soil, knowing that for everything there is a season. In choosing to do this, I help my mother move on, as she has given me life, has helped me grow, and will continue her help as I move through the life cycle.

Nancy:

This is to signify that for a woman biological fertility is one way of fulfilling her creative potential, but there are satisfying challenges in the next phase of life. These trees are planted close enough to each other so that the branches will be entwined. Like a tree, may I stand firmly grounded while the life process helps me branch out in new directions over space and across time. I pray that I will remain fruitful in spirit, mind, and deed and be able to reach meaningfully from my essence to that which is most human in others.

All:

May the roots of the trees spread down deep and wide, into the hidden and mysterious depths of the earth. May they draw up the vital sap of life. May the Shekhinah, praised be She, pour down the precious water of the depths on all who have joined in this healing today. May the rings of these trees bear witness to the power at each of our centers which radiates from core outward. May we continue to open out in the eternal light of God, praised be She.

Nancy:

(I then say a few words about the journey that led me to this [literally ground breaking] ceremony and make a commitment to *tikkun olam*.)

A friend sings *Eitz Chaim* (celebrating the tree of life).

Another friend starts the dancing. We begin to dance with traditional steps and then express our own steps to represent the uniqueness of every soul and the importance of freedom of individual expression.

With the sound of the shofar, we invite my husband and the other men, who have been entertaining the children and organizing the potluck dinner indoors, to join us in the garden.

We end with a story about Lilith and Eve (from *Miriam's*

Well, pp. 23-24), and a prayer for the future, so that these myths can be integrated in the lives of women who can express freely their thoughts and perceptions.

All:

May we live to see the words of the prophets fulfilled: "Then the light of the moon will be like the light of the SUN, and the light of the SUN will be sevenfold, as the light of the seven days. In that day the break of Her people will be bound up and the bruise of their wound healed."

Sh'ma Yisroel, Adonai Elohenu, Adonai Ehad.

Hear O Israel, The Lord Our God, The Lord is One.

Nancy Helman Shneiderman

Exorcising the *Get:* A Ritual of Healing

This past year, while engaged in a spiritual exercise, I discovered that my body, psyche, and soul still held within them an old pain: the pain of my divorce, which had taken place over ten years ago in Israel. In the exercise, I found myself standing alone, unaccustomedly quiet, my feet firm on the ground. Then my arms rose and the palms of my hands opened flat, toward the ceiling. An inner voice told me that even my thumbs had to lie flat. As I stood like that, memory washed over me and I realized I was reliving the experience of the *get*. My belly was burning with a sense of humiliation that ten years ago I never knew I felt.

The experience shocked me: the divorce, after all, was a thing of the past, and in 1987 I had remarried. I hadn't known I still bore the bruises of the *get* ceremony—nor did I realize how profoundly humiliating an experience that *get* ceremony had been. To undergo the ceremony and thus to be legally divorced in the eyes of Israel, where in 1970 we had married, I had returned to the Negev city of Beersheba, our former home. By the time we were ready to go through with the divorce, the pain of our severance had lessened, if not healed. At least neither of us questioned that the time had come for the divorce.

In Israel it is the Orthodox Rabbinate to which one must go, and it is their ritual of divorce which one must undergo. The Beersheba Rabbinate is housed in a dusty old stone building, built by the Turks. We showed the Rabbinical officials our identity cards, marriage certificate, and *ketubah,* and while the scribe wrote out the bill of divorcement—the *get*—according to ancient prescription, we drank espressos with tearful eyes in a local cafe. Hours later they were ready for us; we were ushered into the inner chambers where, cloaked in black, high on the bench above us like judges, the Rabbis sat. How many Rabbis were there I couldn't say—what memory does conjure up for me, though, is that one of them seemed to be nodding off, bored to near sleep.

And my costume, yes my *costume,* comes back to me, too: feeling strange in the heat, the head scarf hiding my hair, as they insisted; the skirt to my ankles; the long sleeves. Who was this woman dressed as if from another time, in this stony place, standing before these men who addressed only my husband and looked quickly away from me?

"And are you agreeing to this from your own free will? free of any pressure?" they asked him in their Yiddish-inflected Hebrew. For an instant I feared he would say, "No, I never wanted this, she wanted this, it's all her fault, I tried my best, make us stay married, make her come back. . . ." But he didn't, he said, "Yes." They nodded and handed him the *get.* The divorcing ritual could begin.

"Stand face to face," they said. "You, *g'veret,* put up your hands, no, not like that, your thumbs are up, you see they show eagerness that way, they mustn't show eagerness, yes, like that, absolutely flat, they have to be flat. Now, *Adoni,* say the words, *'Ha-ray aht megurehshet lee*—Behold you are divorced from me.' " And my husband and I stared straight into one another's eyes, and he said, *"Ha-ray aht megurehshet lee,"* and echoing in my ears were the words of marriage, *"Ha-ray aht mekudehshet lee*—Behold you are sanctified to me," and the Rabbi said, "Now, *Adoni,* drop the *get* into her hands, keep your thumbs down, *g'veret,* absolutely flat, *g'veret,*" and he dropped the *get* into my hands. Still I was silent, still I said nothing, and the Rabbi said, "Now you, *g'veret,* hold the *get* up high, you are showing it to the world, *g'veret,* good, now walk to the four corners of the room holding up the *get,* to that corner, and to that corner," and I held up the *get* high for the world to see, and I marched like a shtetl woman to the four corners of the room, arms outstretched. The Rabbi was pleased and he said, "Come here." I went to the bench and stood before the Rabbis, and one ripped a corner of the *get* and said, "You are free to remarry."

I didn't know then—I didn't know until years later in the room in Los Angeles—that being forced into silence, being forbidden to speak, being rendered unutterably passive, even my thumbs forced down, being made to receive the words, *"Ha-ray aht megurehshet lee,"* made me feel I was being divorced from the good, from the holy, from the sacred, from life itself, humiliated—oh, humiliated so—made me feel I was being punished for seeking an end to the marriage, made me feel thrust into hell.

And that is what, for women, the Orthodox divorce ritual probably was intended to do.

Not until I relived the *get* ceremony in my spiritual exercise did I awaken to my buried pain, did I come face to face with the humiliation for women written into the ceremony, did I realize the price I had paid. I knew if I were to free myself from its impact on me, I had to create a ritual of exorcism. I needed to exorcise the *get.*

The Ritual of Exorcism

And so, on Memorial Day weekend 1990, I gathered together with a group of women for the exorcism. An inner voice I have learned to trust told me the way to do it was to replay what had been. . . dismembering its parts. Every step in the original ceremony needed to be undone: the questioning by the Rabbi; the writing of the *get;* the words of divorce; the march around the room; the ripping of the document; the declaration of freedom.

Women in Orthodox Judaism are not permitted to serve as witnesses: women in my divorce exorcism were my witnesses. A close friend stood in as "Rabbi"; this time around, she asked *me* why *I* wanted the divorce. Standing face to face with her, in words that had been pent up in me for too many years, I spoke the truth of my former marriage as I had experienced it. Then I "read out" my own *get.* When I had said all I needed to say, I pronounced the words I had needed so long ago to be free to pronounce:

Ha-ray ahtah megurash lee

Behold, *you* are divorced from *me.*

And then I strode to the "corners" of the open field, surrounded by sunlit hills, where we had gathered. I declared my right to divorce that which had sapped the strivings of my own soul, psyche, and heart, and had lessened my own capacity for loving and being loved. Returning to the semicircle in which my women witnesses stood, I took the *get, my get,* and I ripped it to shreds. I stomped on the shreds and invited all the witnesses who also bore old rage to name the source of their rage and stomp on the shreds as well.

The ritual was dramatic, powerful, leaving many of us—and certainly me—shaken. But one more time it brought home to me that the awakening of Jewish women in this culture is creating a matrix in which we are free to reclaim the power of, and the right to, our own spiritual lives. In this sense, as in others, the ritual of exorcising the *get* became a needed ritual of healing.

Miriyam Glazer, Ph.D.

Jewish Divorce

"A man takes a wife and possesses her. She fails to please him because he finds something obnoxious about her, and he writes her a bill of divorcement, hands it to her, and sends her away from his house." This verse, Deuteronomy 24:1, provides the basis for divorce according to Jewish law or *Halachah*. It means that there is no divorce other than by way of the husband delivering to the wife—and not vice versa—a bill of divorcement, or a *get*.

Although I consider myself a traditionalist in many ways, I have always taken issue with Judaism's lack of concern for women's equality with men in many aspects of Jewish law. As a Conservative Jew, I applaud the fact that this branch of Judaism has finally dealt with many issues concerning women's participation in the ritual, and particularly those issues concerning the ordination of female rabbis and cantors within the movement. One issue, however, that I take exception with is the inequity concerning the *get,* or Jewish divorce.

I have yet to meet a woman who felt comfortable with the divorce procedure as prescribed by Jewish law. I personally found the experience lonely and humiliating to me as a woman. I do not object to the various aspects of the procedure, such as the scribing of the document, its presentation, tearing of the edges of the document, and so forth, as these aspects all fall under the *Halachah*. What I do object to is the lack of concern for the human soul, the lack of compassion which is so fundamental to our Jewish tradition.

I am, therefore, suggesting a small ceremony which could take place following the traditional ceremony for divorce.

Ceremony

It is important that your closest friends be present. In fact, it would be emotionally supportive to have a good friend accompany you to the actual presentation of the *get*.

Symbols for Ceremony

Salt water — to symbolize the tears shed during this period of mourning.
Egg — traditionally associated with mourning, but also the symbol of life, birth, fertility, and regeneration. The egg is one of nature's strongest structures, yet can be broken easily—as can humankind.
Half-filled goblet of wine — to ask ourselves: "Is life half empty or half filled?"...The choice is ours.

The blessing over the wine is recited to reaffirm our faith in G-d, with the hope that we will find the strength to make the right decisions in our lives.

Hold the half-filled goblet of wine and say:

> *Baruch Ata Adonoy eloheynu melech haolam, boray p'ree hagafan.*
>
> Blessed are You, Lord our G-d, King of the Universe, Who created the fruit of the vine.

In the presence of my dearest friends, I pray that I will find the ability to face the future with a new spirit. I am grateful for the good years that were shared with another human being, and for the children [if there are any] that were formed from this union. May I always remember that with my dear friends and family, and with You, my Maker, that I will never really be alone...and that one day, this goblet of wine will overflow.

Dip the egg into the salt water and eat it. By doing so, you are combining the symbol of tears (salt water) and the symbol of life and regeneration (egg). These are primal emotions associated with both despair and hope for the future.

A small festive meal with friends may follow.

Cantor Judith Bender

Hafradah: A Jewish Separation Ceremony

I wrote this ritual as a part of a course in life-cycle liturgy offered at the Reconstructionist Rabbinical College in 1986. Although I was physically living in Philadelphia during that period of my life, my psychological center was on the west coast, where I had always lived, and which held my lover, family, social network, and career ties. I spent as much time in California as I could manage without doing irreparable damage to my academic standing, so for me, this time held one painful parting after another.

In the course of those years, I was struck by how difficult each single separation was, and how little traditional wisdom existed to guide me in easing the disruptive and depressing emotional after-effects of the many visits and vacations across country. In addition, I realized that my final leave-taking, in June, would bring not only the joy of returning home, but also its own loss of my east coast friends and community. It became clear to me that I wanted a Jewish ritual process with which to deal with my feelings.

I searched Jewish sources for material on separation: stories, rites, philosophic statements, Biblical accounts: Eve and Adam's expulsion from Eden; Abraham's separation from Lot; Jacob and Joseph's departures from their families; Orpah's withdrawal from Naomi; Moses' seculsion from the people of Israel. I looked over Midrashic stories and Kabbalistic explanations of *havdalah,* the separation ceremony between Shabbat and the weekdays.

I wanted a model which was not fault-finding or blaming, which valued what had been and what was to be, while honoring the sadness of transition and loss. The central activity of the ritual is drawn from the story of the parting of Jacob and Laban in Genesis 31. Much of the liturgical and symbolic material is drawn from Kabbalistic (mystical) celebrations of *havdalah.* In the Genesis story, God tells Jacob to leave Laban's camp, where he has lived for twenty years with Leah, Rachel, Bilhah, Zilpah, and their children. The household flees in the night, without saying farewell to Laban, Rachel's and Leah's father. Laban pursues them and confronts Jacob. He says:

> Why did you flee in secrecy and mislead me and not tell me? I would have sent you off with music, with timbrel and lyre. You did not even let me kiss my sons and daughters goodbye. It was a foolish thing for you to do.

The men agree to build a pillar of stones as a witness to a more proper farewell.

This is the part of the tale used in the ritual. Stones are a good material symbol of the significance of such abstract things as relationships. A pillar of stones serves to solidify the metaphoric time of leave-taking; the rocks remain as a physical witness to the importance of the relationship even after the people have had to depart.

Stones are a common religious symbol. Sacred rocks, mounds, and pillars exist in virtually every human culture and spiritual system. In Hawaii there is a folk practice of building small heaps of pebbles on the heights overlooking the Pacific Ocean to serve as homes for wandering spirits. Jews leave small stones at gravesites to show that a visitor has been there. Even God is referred to metaphorically as *Tzur Yisrael,* the Rock of Israel.

The Ritual

This ritual works well for one to about a dozen celebrants. It is designed to pay respect and allow emotional release when one is to be separated from those one loves. The ritual takes place at sunset. It requires a *havdalah* candle, several sectioned apples, ten to thirty small pebbles, a small bottle of glue, some fragrant spices (sage is excellent), a little wine or juice, and enough raisin cakes or bread to feed the participants.

Celebrants gather and hum, chant, or sing *niggunim* outdoors as the sun sets and they prepare to enter sacred time.

The *havdalah* candle is lit and all say:

> *Nevarech makor hechaim, boray m'oray ha-aysh.*
>
> We bless the source of life, Creator of the light of fire.
>
> *Samchuni ba'ashishot.*
>
> Sustain me with lights. (Song of Songs 2:5)

The participants set out the cakes, apples, and stones on a cloth.

Sing a song (possibly "Changes," by Phil Ochs).

Pour the cup of wine or juice.

> *Nevarech makor hechaim, boray p'ree ha-gafen.*

We bless the source of life, Creator of the fruit of the vine.

Reader:

When our ancestors Jacob and Laban parted, they built a mount of stones to stand as a witness to their relationship and separation. We now follow their tradition.

Participants pick up several stones each. As the first person places her/his stone, she/he tells about a memory or feeling associated with the relationship or leave-taking. Each person then does this until all the stones are placed into a mound (a little glue helps), and each person feels satisfied that her/his part of the story has been sufficiently told. This part of the ritual should be given plenty of time, for it is the opportunity to establish continuity and express emotions.

After the mound is built, each participant says:

Ha-gal ha-zeh ayd baynee u'vayn (aych)/(cha) ha-yom.

This stone mound is a witness between me and you this day. (Gen. 31:48)

Yeetzef Adonai baynee u'vayn (aych)/(cha) kee (neestarah)/(neesatar) (isha)/(ish) may-ray'ay (hah)/(hu).

The Eternal will watch between me and you when we are absent from one another. (Gen. 31:49)

Sing a song (possibly "Turn, Turn, Turn," by Pete Seeger).

As participants prepare to drink the wine or juice and eat the apples and raisin cakes, they say:

> *Samchunee ba-asheeshot; rafdoonee ba-tapoocheem.*
>
> Sustain me with raisin cakes; refresh me with apples. (Song of Songs 2:5)

Celebrants eat and drink and say in unison:

> *Nevarech b'vo'aynu, nevarech b'tzaytaynu.*
>
> We bless our comings in and our goings out. (Adapted from Deut. 28:6)

The *havdalah* candle is extinguished in the wine/juice cup.

Reader:

> In ancient times, as in our own, the kiss was a sign of love, respect, and farewell. In the tradition of Laban, Rachel, and Leah; of Orpah and Naomi; of David and Jonathan; we say goodbye and God bless with a kiss.

Everyone kisses and cries.

Rabbi Jane Litman

Sharing a Final Passage

Four months before his thirty-eighth birthday, my brother John died of cancer. We were eighteen months apart in age, he the second and I the first of five siblings. Once I left home to attend college, we never again lived in the same city. Our connection, though, remained as tightly twisted as weathered sisal twine.

During the last few months of John's life, and especially following his death, the colors of my life went wild, and I found myself careening between a profound sense of isolation and an equally powerful sense of community and comfort. Both the women in my life and my Judaism helped me to deal with my pain. In addition to my family, particularly my sisters and my surviving brother, my women friends shared my rage and the deep sadness of watching a strong and determined individual slip away into the jaws of a relentless degenerative disease.

About a month before John died, shortly before what was to be our last visit with one another, I attended a Jewish women's retreat. There, as part of our *havdalah* ceremony, we included a healing circle. It is difficult for me to ask for help, and I remember that one loving friend actually pushed me into the center of the circle. Invoking the Source of all distinctions, women gently encircled me. With words and song, they reminded me of my own strength even as they encouraged me to share my pain with them. My tears flowed freely, and when I returned to the outer circle, I knew God's presence was among us. The power of our sharing reassured me that John was no longer alone as he traveled the lonely corridor between life and death.

After John died, Judaism provided a structure for our mourning, and I found daily *minyanim* to be a necessary and gentle reminder both of the reality of John's death and of the loving connections he had made in his life. My women friends were with me throughout the difficult passages of funeral and *shiva.* I was especially blessed to spend the week after *shiva* at a mountain retreat with a beloved friend. The clear air, our daily walks, and the soft summer rains helped me to acknowledge the depth of my loss. I began to see that healing, though never complete, would come, slowly.

A month after John's funeral, a group of friends came together in a friend's hot tub and performed a ritual to mark the conclusion of *sheloshim,* the month of mourning that begins with *shiva.* Although I was initially reticent to claim our sacred space for my needs, I was grateful for the opportunity to share yet another step of my journey with women friends. Together we entered the space we have consecrated as our *mikveh* and sang Penina Adelman's gentle song, "*V'Anu matzanu menucha*. . . We have found serenity beneath Shechina's wings." Then Drorah, who acted as the *mesaderet tefila,* the facilitator of the simple ritual, asked me to say a few words about John, about his life, about his death, and about the month of mourning that was now coming to an end. She then asked me to share three memories—three legacies of John's life and of our sibling relationship that I wanted to keep and three that I wanted to leave behind. Her question was unexpected and, initially, difficult for me to answer. But I felt the support of my friends and the comfort of the waters, and I spoke. When I had finished, after a shared silence, I immersed myself three times.

We concluded by singing *"Chazak, chazak, v'nitchazek:* From strength, to strength, we strengthen one another." Faith Rogow's powerful melody gives wings to the ancient words. I felt ready to enter the next stage of my grieving, knowing that there were more tears ahead but that those tears would clear the way to greater understanding.

Now, the months have become years. The love of women remains an essential part of my healing and my life.

Rabbi Sue Levi Elwell

Birkat Ha-Neetzan: Blessing the Blossom
A Celebration of Emerging Womanhood

I lovingly created this ceremony on the occasion of my daughter Tami's becoming a *Neetzan* in July 1988. The ceremony had its origins in a meeting of Isha L'Isha in 1986 when the basic structure of such a ceremony was planned, under the leadership of our facilitator, Marcia Plumb, who is now a rabbi. At that time, none of our daughters was old enough to participate in the ritual, so we patiently waited. The blessing, "Many are the mothers. . ." was written with assistance from Rabbi Jane Litman for Tami's bat mitzvah. Thank you to Jane and to my soul-sisters in Isha L'Isha. We hope this ceremony will be adopted and modified for future celebrations among mothers, daughters, and the community of women.

We read together:

> This evening we come together as women to gently welcome one of our daughters into a new stage in her life. We choose to call this ceremony *Birkat Ha-Neetzan,* Blessing the Blossom. The symbolism of the blossom expresses the essence of a little girl transforming into a young woman, just as a tiny bud matures into a flower.

Washing Our Hands

We begin the *Birkat Ha-Neetzan* by washing each other's hands. As we pass the bowl of water and towel from one woman to another, we symbolically cleanse ourselves, a holy act. We are washing off any negative images we have of ourselves as women, feelings of dirtiness, embarrassment, and discomfort that we may have learned from society. By washing each others' hands, we emerge clean and fresh, knowing that our sexuality is a beautiful part of us. By washing each others' hands, we also form a chain of support for one another as women. So we say the blessing:

> *Baruch Ata Adonai Eloheinu, Melech Ha-olam, asher kideshanu bemitsvotav vetsivanu al netilat yadayim.**
>
> Blessed are you, Eternal our God, Creator of the Universe, who makes us holy by your mitzvot and commands us to wash our hands.

(The mother washes her daughter's hands and face. As preparation for her new role as a young woman, the *Neetzan* repeats the blessing.)

Sharing Our Blossoms

Each woman presents a flower to the *Neetzan* and shares the poems, readings, songs, special thoughts, and memories

---

* Because I believe that God is genderless, or genderful, I have interchanged gender at random and given approximate interpretations rather than direct translations.

she has brought for this evening. The flowers are woven into a crown for the *Neetzan*. The crown is completed when the sharing is finished and the crown is placed upon the head of the *Neetzan*.

Tami recites the following blessings:

Bruchah At ha-Shechina she'astani isha.

I bless the Source of Life, who has created me a woman.

We all say:

Baruch Ata Adonai Eloheinu Melech Ha-olam shehhechiyanu, v'kiyamanu, v'higiyanu, lazman hazeh.

Blessed are You, Holy one of Being, Parent of us all, who has brought us with great joy to this moment in Tami's life and in the lives of all of us joined in celebration.

Bruchah At ha-Shechina she'astani isha.

Songs of Womanhood

Leche Lach
Erev Shel Shoshanim
Woman I Am
Dodi Li

Other songs as desired by the group

Foods of Blossoming

Now we partake of symbolic foods and participate in feeding the *Neetzan:*

Red wine for joyous celebration.

> *Baruch Ata Adonai Eloheinu Melech Ha-olam,*
> *borei p'ri ha-gafen.*
>
> We bless the Source of Life, who has given us the sweet, red fruit of the vine.

Round Challah with raisins for sweetness and rising—a gradual growing, and the feminine shape of blossoming fertility.

> *Baruch Ata Adonai Eloheinu Melech Ha-olam*
> *ha-motzi lechem meen ha-aretz.*
>
> We bless the Source of Life which creates bread from the Earth as She creates the power of life within us.

Raspberries, strawberries, watermelon, other red fruits for ripening, for blossoming, for beauty and femininity, for future fruitfulness, and for the variety of experiences that await you.

> *Baruch Ata Adonai Eloheinu Melech Ha-olam*
> *boray p'ri ha-eytz.*
>
> We bless the Source of Life that causes us to experience our feminine beauty.

We bless the Source of Life that enables us, like the fruit, to ripen.

From Mother to Daughter

We say together:

Many are the mothers, numerous are the daughters who have shaped our people.

Blessed be the mothers, blessed be the daughters.

May you, Tami, daughter of Israel, be like them:
patient, as Sarah
gracious, like Rebecca
nurturing, as Leah
loving, like Rachel.
(women of Torah)

May you be...
devoted, as Ruth
dignified, like Naomi
faithful, as Miriam
determined, like Tamar.
(biblical women)

May you be...
heroic, as Judith
wise, like Bruria
generous, as Gracia Mendes
compassionate, like Emma Lazarus.
(post-biblical women)

May you be...
responsible, as Lillian Wald
assertive, like Golda Meir
courageous, as Hannah Senesh
hopeful, like Anne Frank.
(20th century women)

Mother:

We light two pink candles that were first lit at your *Brit Ha-Nerot* ceremony when you were a baby. We make a link with your beginning as a Jewish girl while we also anticipate your future as a Jewish woman.

(Mother and daughter each light a pink candle.)

Mother:

We light this red candle to symbolize this new stage in your life as a *Neetzan,* a blossom. Red reminds us of the brilliant color of the life force; fire reminds us of the power you now share with all women everywhere. Through the struggles of this stage in your life, may you learn to use this power in goodness.

(Mother and daughter each take a pink candle and together light the red candle.)

Together:

Baruch Ata Adonai Eloheinu Melech Ha-olam,
asher kideshanu bemitzvotav vetsivanu l'hadleek
ner shel ha-neetzan.

Silent Meditation for the Blossom

Prior to the ceremony, the *Neetzan,* alone or with her mother, may want to write a meditation.

Conclusion: "My blessing for you is..."

We form our closing circle. Each woman passes around the red candle and gives her one word blessing to the *Neetzan*. The mother gives her blessing last and passes the candle to the *Neetzan.* The *Neetzan* says thank you in any manner she chooses. We all sing our closing song:

> *Hiney ma tov uma naim shevet achiyot gam yachad.*
>
> Behold how good and how pleasant it is for sisters to dwell together!

Barbara Kochman Singer

A Commitment Celebration

We decided to formalize our lifelong commitment for many reasons, the foremost of which was our intention to have children. We saw the ceremony as an opportunity for friends and relatives to consciously acknowledge us as a family and commit to becoming our allies in making the world a safer and more supportive place for us and our children. We also did it as an act of liberation, for our right and the right of gay people everywhere to live openly and authentically. We believe that the process of winning human rights begins when oppressed people start acting *as if* we had those rights. Holding a public commitment ceremony was our way of "taking a seat at the front of the bus."

Our ceremony was structured around the affirmation of four covenants:

1. with the world (both the natural world and all of humanity),
2. with our face-to-face communities,
3. with our families, and
4. with each other.

Each covenant was introduced and explained, and then symbolized by some act: the reading of a poem, the giving of blessings, the sharing of fruits, and the reading of the *ketubah*. (Prior to the ceremony, we met with family members for a private signing of the *ketubah* and to show them the legal documents we had drawn up to protect our relationship in the secular world.)

The ceremony took place outdoors before seventy guests at the home of friends. It began with the raising of the *huppah,* a patchwork quilt made from squares created for us by family and friends. Our brothers and two friends held the poles. The ceremony was facilitated by three close women friends, two of whom happen to be rabbis, but who did not officiate as such. As we entered, the facilitators led the guests in singing a song written by Shefa Gold:

> May we always remember where we come from
> May we see the whole in every part
> May Her blessings pour down on everyone
> As love pours from my heart.[1]

Our friend Joanna introduced the program, talking about how we create holy space when we gather together with *kavanah*, and how witnessing this ceremony was an act of commitment to uphold our covenant. Then our friend Merle spoke about our covenant with the world and our desire to live in the spirit of *tikkun olam,* to heal and repair the world through our commitment to ecology, peace, and social justice. Moon's mother read the invocation, a poem by e e cummings about the presence of God in the natural world.

Our friend Julie introduced our covenant with community as a holy *massa u'matan,* the flow of energy that occurs when we give and receive the fruits of each other's work and caring. Then each of the seven individuals or couples we had asked came forward and gave us their blessing. This idea was inspired by the traditional *sheva brachot*.

For our covenant with our families, we each spoke in turn

about the joys and struggles of building family relationships that are open and real, and rededicated ourselves to that process. We invited our family members and women's group to stand beside us as we blessed a tray of chocolate covered strawberries,[2] which we first served to our families and then passed around to everyone present as a way of giving back the blessings we had received and sharing the sweetness with them.

The fourth covenant, with each other, was introduced by our friends Shira and Carol, reading from a lovely translation of the *Song of Songs* by Marcia Falk. Julie read the introductory paragraph of our *ketubah,* and we, in turn, read our promises to one another. We recited the final lines from the *Book of Ruth* together, placed the rings on our own fingers (to show that we were not being purchased or given, but entering freely into the covenant), and kissed.

We stepped out from under the *huppah* into the embrace of family and friends. After the ceremony, everyone was invited to the house to break bread together and to enjoy a vegetarian buffet lunch, hugs, photos, and the final signing of the *ketubah.*

All seventy witnesses were invited to sign the *ketubah.* Our *ketubah* was hand-crafted by artist/calligrapher Susan Leviton[3] and was written and signed in nonfading ink for permanent display in our home.

The words of our *ketubah* are:

> On the 5th day of Av, 5749, which is the 6th day of August, 1989, Moon Elizabeth Smith and Susan Edith Saxe made this covenant under the wings of the Shechinna and in the circle of our community:
>
> I will live with you as your faithful partner.

I will support and uphold you in abundance and in adversity.

I will encourage you to grow to your fullest potential and I will take responsibility for my own growth and well-being.

I promise to reach deep within myself, even when it is most difficult, to be fully present, honest, trusting, patient, and compassionate with you.

I will build with you a loving home and share with you the joys and responsibilities of creating and nurturing our family.

I will strive with you to live in the spirit of *Tikkun Olam,* responsibly, with openness and respect toward our families, our diverse communities, and the natural world.

"Where you go, I will go. Where you live, I will live. Your people will be my people and your God my God."

Moon Smith and Susan Saxe

---

[1] From her audio cassette, *Songs of Renewal and Jubilation.* Her tapes can be ordered by writing to her c/o Rose Mountain, P. O. Box 355, Las Vegas, NM 87701.

[2] We chose strawberries as a "fruit of the vine," because, after some thought, we had decided to have a totally alcohol-free event. This felt like a very life-affirming statement in light of the oppressive role alcohol can play in the lives of

individuals and communities. If anything, this decision added to the joy of the day.

[3] c/o Levworks, 3417 North 4th Street, Harrisburg, PA 17110, (717) 236-0231.

Ceremony Upon Becoming a Vegetarian

I wrote this ceremony when I took a class called "Creating Sacred Ceremonies for Jewish Women," taught by Irene Fine in January/February 1989. When Irene told us that each of us was to write a ceremony by the end of the class, my thoughts turned to writing a ceremony about becoming a vegetarian. At the time I still ate fish, although I had given up meat several years before. I had been leaning toward becoming a vegetarian, and this seemed to be the time. Taking the class and having to write a ceremony propelled me into taking the next step. I have (happily) remained a vegetarian since that time.

Opening

> God said, "See, I give you every seed-bearing plant that is upon all the earth, and every tree that has seed-bearing fruit; they shall be yours for food. And to all the animals on land, to all the birds of the sky, and to everything that creeps on earth, in which there is the breath of life, [I give] all the green plants for food." And it was so. (Genesis 1:29-30)

Our tradition teaches that at the beginning of time, in the perfect society (Gan Eden), we were vegetarians. Only after the Flood does the Torah say that we were given permission to eat meat. Many have seen this as a divine concession to human weakness. We no longer live in Gan Eden. But the prophet Isaiah writes that at the end of time, in the messianic age, the world will return to vegetarianism.

> The wolf shall dwell with the lamb,
> The leopard lie down with the kid;
> The calf, the beast of prey, and the fatling
> together,
> With a little child to herd them.
> The cow and the bear shall graze,
> Their young shall lie down together;
> And the lion, like the ox, shall eat straw.
> (Isaiah 11:6-7)

Statement of Intent or Purpose (Naming)

I believe that our task in life is *tikkun olam*—to help mend the world—to bring the messianic age closer. "It is not incumbent upon us to complete the task, but neither are we free to desist from it." (Pirke Avot 2:21)

A few years ago I stopped eating meat. I continued, though, to eat fish. Lately I have begun to feel slightly uncomfortable about eating fish. The rabbis of the Talmud taught that we should not eat meat unless we crave it, and then only occasionally and sparingly (Chulin 84a). Several months ago, I took this approach to eating fish. And I found that while I *enjoyed* fish on occasion, I didn't *crave* it. I can get along perfectly well without eating fish. The protein I can get from other sources. Why, then, take a life unnecessarily?

> Fear not, you beasts of the field
> For the pastures of the wilderness

Are green
The tree bears its fruit
The fig tree and vine yield their strength.
(Joel 2:22)

Along the path of *tikkun olam,* therefore, my next step—and one that seems quite natural—is to stop eating fish (as well as meat). I now call myself a vegetarian.

Articulation of What is Lost and What is Gained

What have I lost in becoming a vegetarian? Well, I have given up the tastes of meat and fish. I have also made it more difficult for my friends and family to invite me to their homes for dinner. Now they have to consider my special needs, and I did not become a vegetarian to impose these requirements on others. Finally, I have had to become a careful label reader. All kinds of packaged foods that seem quite innocuous actually contain animal products. What have I lost? Hours of free time in the supermarket!

Except for the difficulties presented to family and friends, these losses pale in comparison to the gains I reap in becoming a vegetarian. For one thing, I am able to practice *kashrut* as I feel it really is intended, and that is to learn and exhibit reverence for the sanctity of life. How better to demonstrate this reverence than by refraining from killing an animal or fish to eat its flesh? I also feel I am doing a (very) small part in conserving the earth's resources. A flesh-centered diet wastes food and other valuable resources and contributes to pollution and the malnutrition and starvation of others. Finally, as a vegetarian, I feel healthier and less polluted myself. For spiritual, religious, humane, people- and animal-loving, environmental, and health reasons, I am glad to become a vegetarian.

Prayer / Blessing

(Original) Blessing Upon Becoming a Vegetarian

Blessed is the Source of Life
Spring of Sustenance
Who causes fruit to ripen on the branch
And bread to come forth from the earth.

In your lovingkindness and magnanimity
O, Womb of the Universe
Nest of Creation
You have given us for nourishment
Every seed-bearing plant that is upon the earth
And every tree that has seed-bearing fruit
These to be ours for food.

Morning, noon, and night we partake of Your
bounty
And behold, it is good.

Help us now to hunger and thirst for You
To value Your gifts, and to walk in Your ways
To revere life and not to take it needlessly
To be worthy of all You have given us.

O, Well of Sustenance
Support me as I travel this vegetarian path
Nourish me, body and soul
With an awareness of Your closeness.

B'rucha Yah Shechinah, Ma'yan Chayim
Blessed are You, Compassionate Source of Life
Shehecheyatnu

Who has given us life
V'kiyy'matnu
And sustained us
V'higgiatnu
And brought us
laz'zman hazeh
To this time.

Activity — Eating

Recite the appropriate blessings* and drink wine and eat fruits and vegetables. Especially appropriate are foods mentioned in the Torah: apples, oranges, dates, figs, pomegranates, carobs, almonds, nuts, honey. (I don't like olives!) An apple with honey, for a sweet "beginning" (*a la* Rosh Ha-Shanah), is also appropriately symbolic.

---

*Blessings (I use the feminine form—*Shechinah*—to emphasize God's motherly, nurturing attributes):

B'rucha Yah Shechinah, Ma'yan Chayim, borayt p'ri hagafen.

Blessed are You, God, Source/Spring of Life, Who creates the fruit of the vine.

B'rucha Yah Shechinah, Ma'yan Chayim, borayt p'ri ha-etz.

Blessed are You, God, Source/Spring of Life, Who creates the fruit of the tree.

B'rucha Yah Shechinah, Ma'yan Chayim, borayt p'ri ha-adama.

Blessed are You, God, Source/Spring of Life, Who creates the fruit of the earth.

Contribution to *tzedakah* (perhaps plant a fruit-bearing tree)

Song

Elizabeth Resnick Levine

Celebrating Rabbinic Ordination

Naming our women teachers is an important step in the process of Jewish feminist empowerment. We have so many different kinds of teachers: mothers, wise women, professors, sisters in struggle, etc. They all deserve to be named and honored.

One relatively new role for women is the role of rabbi. In the past fifteen years, over one hundred women have graduated from rabbinical seminaries and at least a dozen others have received private ordination. As these women become our teachers, we need new ceremonies to acknowledge their role in our lives. We also might want to follow the suggestion of Rabbi Jane Litman that we look to our history for Jewish women leaders who could not receive the title "Rabbi" in their own time and bequeath that title upon them today.

I have been part of four feminist ordination ceremonies in which communities of women have celebrated and affirmed the entry of individual women into the rabbinate. Each ceremony was unique and was designed with the particular woman in mind. In some cases the woman helped plan her own ceremony, in others it was planned for her. In each case, the essence of the ritual was what the group of women brought to the format, rather than the format itself.

As with any good ritual, these ceremonies created space for the feelings, ideas, bodies, and interactions of the people present. They are not rote formulas that can be transmitted regardless of who will be present. The presence of beloveds, and their contributions, made these rituals work.

One ordination ceremony took place at a Jewish feminist retreat attended by over twenty friends who were all active in the Jewish world. Sue Levi Elwell and Sheila Peltz Weinberg would be ordained by the Reform and Reconstructionist movements, respectively, within the next few weeks. The ceremony took place at Havdalah time, to mark the distinction of the next step for Sheila and Sue, while affirming the continuity of friendship, of sisterhood, and of Jewish leadership.

We gathered together shoulder-to-shoulder in a circle in the sanctuary. Inside the circle Sue and Sheila walked from woman to woman, receiving a blessing from each for the journey forward into the rabbinate. Then they both spoke about what it meant to them to become a rabbi.

Sheila remembers, "I felt Sue and I were embodying a movement of women into the tradition. I knew from then on I'd have a strong relationship to the tradition, and I really wanted the blessing of the women. It was very powerful. I wanted reassurance and to reassure that I wasn't going to be abandoned or abandon. I didn't want to go out and be like all rabbis, overwhelmed by the way things have always been."

Sue recalls, "There were lots of tears. There's a power in tears: as we transmit we are also transforming. I also remember Rabbi Susan Harris standing in the circle (she had been ordained the year before), saying to me 'when you're ordained, the head of your seminary will put his hands on your shoulders, but you don't have to look down. Look him in the eye.' I stood up there two weeks later and looked him straight in the eye. She emboldened me."

At another ordination ceremony a circle of six close

women friends came together to weave a crown of beauty for Joanna Katz shortly before her graduation from the Reconstructionist Rabbinical College. Joanna spoke about the tremendous support she had received from her feminist friends during her years in a patriarchal rabbinical seminary. We each made a wish for her well-being in the rabbinate and wove it into the crown. Then we bedecked her with the gorgeous ring of dried flowers, grasses, ribbons, and other treasures. It hangs on her wall to this day.

A year later, twenty-five friends and three of my four sisters gathered to ordain me as Rabbi on the eve of my graduation from the Reconstructionist Rabbinical College. The ceremony was held at night in a circle outside, lit by lantern light. Each woman spoke of the ways in which I had been a teacher for her. When her turn came, my sister Miggie said, "I've known Julie for thirty-two years and the first thing I remember her teaching me was how to spell *milk!*" I felt my past and my future meeting.

Then various women rose to prepare me to take the journey into the rabbinate. They washed my feet, anointed me, and presented me with a beautiful woven tallis. We closed with everyone laying her hands on me (the traditional form of ordination is called *smikha* in which the teacher lays his hands on the student and the student is declared to be a rabbi) and singing.

Then we all had hot fudge sundaes! I remember glowing, basking in the endorsement of these beloveds, ready to go out and face the not-always-welcoming world of the rabbinate.

The fourth ceremony was planned by Rabbi Joanna Katz and myself for Elana Schachter-Shalomi, who was receiving private rabbinic ordination from the Hassidic rebbe Shlomo Carlebach. We wanted to create a document for her, acknowledging her as our teacher. To find a relevant biblical quotation, we started by looking in the concordance (a book that lists every word in the Bible with its references) under the word *Elana,* which means "tree" in Hebrew. We quickly found a passage in Daniel (4:8) that said, "The tree grew and was strong, and its top reached to the sky, and it was visible to the end of all the earth." That seemed perfect, especially since the Hebrew word for "grew and was strong" is *rava,* a feminine form of rabbi. Thus, in Hebrew, the passage actually started with "Rabbi Elana."

We commissioned artist Betsy Teutsch to create a document depicting a tree with Elana's Hebrew name woven into the branches surrounded by the quote from Daniel. We left ten lines at the bottom for a *minyan* of signatures. Then we invited twenty-five of Elana's friends to join us. First, we had a study session on several selections from Torah, including one about Deborah, who was a judge and rabbi. Elana taught and we also went around the circle creating our own *midrash* on the lines.

Then we each lit a candle and spoke of the ways in which Elana, as a teacher, had brought light to our lives. And finally we laid hands on her in *smikha* and presented the document.

In these four ceremonies, a horizontal process of affirmation, rather than a top-down process of judgment, took place. Traditionally, the teachers of one generation pass down the title "Rabbi" to their students in the next generation. The teacher does this in the presence of a *Beyt Din* or Court of Law. We created a circle in which peers acknowledge the strength of a sister, publicly proclaiming her to be a teacher of Torah in the broadest sense. So far we have done this only for women who have also taken a path formally legitimized by rabbinic institutions. What would it mean for Jewish feminists to create our own ordination process, independent of the major rabbinical institutions and personalities? That is an idea whose time may have come.

Rabbi Julie Greenberg

Eshet Hazon: A Woman of Vision

Do you remember the television show, "Queen for a Day"? As a young girl, I remember watching that program and thinking how magical it would feel to be honored and chosen, even though most of the prizes were household appliances which didn't interest me. My fascination with royalty has led me on a long road of dreams of glory, only to discover that She, whom I was seeking, dwells within me. It was on the 8th of Sivan, 5742 — May 30, 1982 — that I and others formally acknowledged that Indwelling Presence.

I was living with my family in Vancouver, B.C., and was helping to give birth to a new havurah, called Or Shalom. Through Rosh Hodesh gatherings, we boldly explored where very few Jewish women had gone before and began to offer our new-found strength in the formation of a community of spiritually seeking men and women. Our stories were told and our creativity soared. We gathered at times with other women in the spectacular beauty and receptivity of the Pacific Northwest and began to realize that we were part of a purposeful renewal of the Jewish people.

In 1982, I began to organize a Shavuot Retreat for the Northwest Havurot, to be held at Camp Solomon Schechter in Olympia, Washington. It was a glorious gathering. The davening was deeply moving and people were brought together through a love of Torah, nature, and a sharing of visions. By Saturday night I was exhausted, and as others danced, I cried, feeling drained and depleted. I went to sleep early and as I slept, others had sacred visions.

The women who knew me were inspired to create a ceremony that acknowledged the work I was doing and the ways in which I had touched their lives. They wanted to empower me with their love, to support my teaching as a woman of intuition and devotion. Being married to a rabbi, I constantly wrestled with my role as his partner and my own unordained spiritual qualities. Yes, I wanted to be a rabbi, too, but life choices had taken me down a road of life experiences rather than seminary credentials.

Sunday morning I awoke and sensed an electric energy charge in the air. As I left my cabin, I was met by Shira Tzipporah who held my arm firmly and escorted me down the grassy hill to a meadow by the lake where about sixty men and women were gathered in a circle with a Torah. They began singing one of the melodies I had written and then centered me beneath a baby blanket I had woven. The ceremony began. I was to be initiated as an *Eshet Hazon,* A Woman of Vision, and a *Miyoledet Shel Neshama,* A Midwife of the Soul.

Michelle from Deadwood cleansed the space with cedar boughs and a large eagle feather. Four of my dearest sisters held the corners of the baby blanket huppah, and my handwoven rainbow poncho tallis was placed over my head. Like a convert, I stood in the consciousness of unworthiness, but the light and power of Sinai began to fill the place of my heart.

A ketubah document was designed by Shonna and Judith with symbols of the rainbow, a lotus, *hamsas,* moon and stars, and a shofar. The text was composed by the all-night women's gathering. My lineage is written in the rainbow—Hanna Tiferet bat Bayla bat Shprinza bat Bayla. And it says:

As the flowers in a springtime bouquet, so too

> do you express your Jewish spirit, vibrant with life's creative forces flowing through you as a river, strong as the mighty Cedars of Lebanon with branches delicately dancing in the breeze. Your ancient wisdom envelops you as a cloud of lilac dust, a fragrance so deep none can ignore. The feminine spirit of the divine Mother lies within you. You give magic form and deep expression, calling forth Jewish women's spirituality through all time. Through dance and music, weavings and birthings, prayer and quiet revelations of learning and sharing, you radiate life's beauty to those around you and serve as a model, guide, and spiritual teacher to many. And so, with the blessings of Shadai, Malkat Olam, queen of the Eternal Presence, we wish to formally acknowledge you, Hanna Tiferet, as a *Miyoledet Shel Neshama* (midwife of the soul) and bestow upon you the title of *Eshet Hazon* (woman of vision) from your havurah. May you be blessed with evergrowing strength and insight to express your vision of the Torah of the hand and heart, and the sensitivity to feel the circle of love and encouragement with which we surround you. Dated this 8th day of Sivan 5742, May 30, 1982, at Camp Solomon Schechter near Olympia, Washington.

Then the "simcha" cup that Shira had fashioned from silver, opals, and amethysts was filled with wine and Shanti chanted a kiddush as only she can do. The cup was passed and friends offered a prayer, a blessing, or a song. Tears flowed from the sorrow of longing and the celebration of fulfillment. It was a moment of eternity, timeless, inspired.

It was Sinai for me, as I stood open to the world and received God's love.

Since that time, much has happened. I continue to wrestle with the issues of power in a world that recognizes titles and degrees. Other women in the United States, Canada, and Israel have received the ordination of *Eshet Hazon* from their sisters in community. Each woman has a second title that is suited to her creative work. Slowly it is taking root. As we discover that we are not powerless and that we can empower each other, the wounds of inadequacy are healed. Many women do receive rabbinic ordination today, yet many great women teachers remain hidden and perhaps discouraged by their lack of recognition. When the light shines, we must notice. As we open our hearts to each other and overcome the jealousy and competition of Sarah and Hagar, we bring healing to this world. When we empower each other with love, we discover the true power of sharing.

Hanna Tiferet Siegel

Hanukah: Lighting the Way to Women's Empowerment

Three Jewish women, Nina, Amy, and Rachel, wanted to transform the commemoration of a military victory into a search for peace. We saw darkness in the Hanukah story as a metaphor for the darkness that feminists feel in the world right now, probably have always felt. We saw the *hanukiah* as a symbol of hope that we can find more light, energy, and power than we expect when we are in personal and spiritual darkness.

We made a deliberate decision to recognize the work of our hands in preparing traditional food as a central part of our celebration. We also chose to honor the voices of women by inviting other women and asking them to participate in a story-telling ritual.

Our ritual started in the kitchen, with communal preparations, the cooking and sharing of latkes and applesauce. We then gathered in the dim light around Rachel's dining table. We were eleven women ranging in age from our twenties to our sixties and four young children. Nicole and Talia had each made a Play-Doh menorah: a circle of flowers in many colors. Each of us lit her own *hanukiah*. With some shyness, we sang the prayers that Nina had brought back from the Banoth Yerushalayim Feminist Liturgy Project.

Barucha At Shehina, Elohateinu Me'irat ha-olam, asher azratnu b'nifla-oteiha v'kidshatnu b'hadlakat ner shel Hanukah.

Blessed are You, Divine Presence, our Goddess Illuminator of the world, who helped us with her wonders and sanctified us through kindling of Hanukah lights.

Barucha At Shehina, Elohateinu Me'irat ha-olam, she'asta nisim l'ameinu bayamim haheim bazman hazeh.

Blessed are You, Divine Presence, our Goddess Illuminator of the world, who worked miracles for our people in those days, at this time.

Holding the bright blue programs that Rachel had made and reading the feminist blessings that we had composed together, we were making new sense out of ancient custom.

We come together to sanctify this day of Hanukah
with our love and respect for each other
and for the universe in which we dwell.
In this cold and darkening winter season
and at this time of deepening conflict and
potential nuclear annihilation,
we kindle the lights of Hanukah
as a symbol of hope
in the pursuit of peace among all people.

May these Hanukah candles unite us
with Jewish women and friends of Jewish women
who have felt oppression and struggled for freedom
each in her own way
in all places and at all times.

We bless that which is human and divine in each
of us
We bless the miracle of life and death
We bless the miracle of a light that shines beyond
despair
We bless the miracle of hope and faith in our
search for peace
We bless the spirit of sisterhood that enables us
To speak our wisdom and our faith in our own
words.

We rejoice and we bless the inspiration, the
strength, and sensitivity
that keep us alive and enable us to celebrate
together
and to reach this season
with willingness to look at the condition of Jewish
women,
to talk about it, and to transform our
victimization
into positive energy, meaningful action, and
creative self-expression.

As the community of women spoke, our words took on a life and power of their own.

We envision our search for peaceful human
solutions
out of the commemoration of a military victory
and out of the miracle of one light
that shines more than we think.

We moved on to the story-telling part of the ritual. We had asked each woman to bring another Jewish woman or group of Jewish women with her in spirit. We told each other about these women. As we spoke, we felt the presence and the colorful diversity of our too often invisible Jewish sisters and mothers, those we had named and those who remained unnamed.

Our ritual-making process can be extended to other holidays also. We began by rewriting the traditional Hanukah blessings. We discarded the male-centered and hierarchical patriarchal images of an external male deity. We reclaimed instead the deity within us. We asserted our individual and collective power to name the events of our Jewish history and of our present reality and to bless our caring, respectful love of our universe and each other.

We see our coming together as women to create new symbols and new ways of celebrating as an essential process toward empowering ourselves as Jewish women in our search for peace and cooperation among all.

Nina Katz, Amy Sheldon,
and Rachel Josefowitz Siegel

(Another version of this ceremony was previously published in *Bridges,* Vol. I, No. 2.)

By Special Invitation: Women's Place at *Sukkot*

On a sunny October afternoon last year, the women of our family gathered around the kitchen table to complete the preparations for Sukkot. The *sukka* had been raised, the pine boughs carefully laid on top. Now baskets of autumn fruits and vegetables—apples, pears, grapes, and fiery red peppers—jostled with one another on the table where we were stringing together *sukka* decorations.

Earlier that afternoon, we'd brought down from the attic our rain-wrinkled *ushpizin,* the traditional invitation extended nightly to each of the biblical patriarchs. Every year we proudly hung the family *ushpizin,* a print made by our Uncle Yitzhak of Jerusalem, in a prominent spot in the *sukka.* This year, pausing a moment to look at the family heirloom, we were struck by disturbing omissions: Where were the women? What about the matriarchs?

Sisters, mother, sister-in-law—we were transformed instantly into a feminist group, torn between anger and the desire to shrug off the nagging questions. Suddenly, one of us suggested, "Why not a women's *ushpizin?*" Indeed, why not?

Brought up in a traditional home and community, we had not before noticed the exclusive character of the traditional *ushpizin.* We had been taught so much about our forefathers, so little of the women in our history. Who were these women? What were their names and their stories? These questions had led our family in recent years to compile a supplement to the Passover Haggada, with songs and readings that spoke of other struggles for liberation, including that of women.

Over the kitchen table, over the chopping of soup vegetables and the stringing of grapes and peppers, we planned our women's *ushpizin*—one which would invite our mothers and sisters into our *sukka*. Animatedly, we called out the names of women from biblical days to the present whom we would honor: Beruriah, Rebekah, Deborah, Gluckel of Hameln, Henrietta Szold, and Hannah Senesh. We reminded each other of women we'd forgotten, teaching ourselves new bits of Jewish women's history: Adrienne Rich, Nellie Sachs. We reached into our own family history, remembering our grandmothers: Miriam, Rachel, Sara, Hannah Devorah, Adel Batya, Frieda, Yetta, and Anna. We argued vehemently over Golda Meir, with Mother insisting, "Golda is a Jewish heroine, whether you like her politics or not."

But all too soon our stock of names was depleted. We realized how many gaps there were in our knowledge—whole centuries unrepresented because we knew nothing of the women who had lived then. For all our years of Jewish education, we had learned of many Jewish men—rabbis, soldiers, diplomats, even athletes—but we could name only a handful of women. How many Jewish women had been silent or silenced, we wondered, their dreams and their visions ignored, their talents suppressed? All the more reason, we felt, to create a women's *ushpizin* to reclaim this half of our history.

Although we looked to the traditional *ushpizin* as a model, we decided to modify its basic concept in one respect. We had no desire to invite only the superstars of Jewish history; we wanted to include the unsung heroines as well in our *sukka*. Our women's *ushpizin* would challenge both the male-dominated view of history and the traditional concept of a hero or heroine. In addition to the biblical matriarchs, we would include those many women who had shaped our values and beliefs, who had served as our role models.

In our invitation, we expressed this view through new categories:

> We now invite to our meal and to our *sukka* those women, our honored mothers and sisters, who have passed on to us over the generations their wisdom and visions, their healing and nurturing, their dreams and daring, their songs and silences. We thank them by continuing in their traditions.

Each night we chose a different group of women to invite:

> On the first night, we invite our first mothers, Lilith and Eve.
>
> On the second night, we invite our matriarchs: Sarah, Rebekah, Leah, and Rachel.
>
> On the third night, we invite our prophetesses and wisewomen: Zipporah, Miriam, Deborah, Naomi, Beruriah, Gracia Nasi, Ima Shalom, Adrienne Rich, and those many women whose names and stories have been denied to us.
>
> On the fourth night, we invite our healers and nurturers: Batya, Shifrah and Puah, Judith Montefiore, Henrietta Szold, Ruth Kluger, the pioneer women of Israel who worked the land, and those many women whose names and stories have been denied to us.

On the fifth night, we invite our dreamers and darers: Dinah, Tamar, Ruth, Esther, Gluckel of Hameln, Emma Lazarus, Emma Goldman, Rosa Luxemburg, Kathe Kollwitz, Muriel Rukeyser, Hannah Senesh, Recha Freier, Bessie Gottsfeld, Shulamith Aloni, the Women at the Wall, Alice Shalvi, Rachel the poet, and those many women whose names and stories have been denied to us.

On the sixth night, we invite our own grandmothers: Miriam, Rachel, Sara, Hannah Devorah, Adel Batya, Frieda, Yetta, and Anna.

On the seventh night, we invite our silent and silenced sisters of all times, those forgotten and those suppressed, those whose names and stories, though unknown, are as important as our own.

All that week, our *ushpizin* was the central focus for those who entered our *sukka.* At a *kiddush* for neighborhood friends, an 80-year-old woman exclaimed over and over how wonderful the *ushpizin* was. Our visitors inundated us with suggestions of other Jewish women we might have included. And again and again we heard, "Why not Golda Meir?"

* * *

One elderly lady who visited our *sukka* told us that the house to which we had recently moved had long been a center of Jewish and Israel-oriented community projects, under the direction of the energetic Jewish women of Buffalo. In the 1930's, she told us, Henrietta Szold had met with a pioneer group of Hadassah women in this same house. "So why not a women's *ushpizin* here?" she asked.

Our rediscovery goes on. Having created a new connection

between Sukkot and ourselves, we can look to the women we invited into our *sukka* and know that we, too, have a tradition of learning and nurturing, dreaming and daring.

Adina Back, Toby Ticktin Back,
Rachel Back, Sara Back, and Tara Blau

(Originally published in *Hadassah Magazine,* October 1982.)

Contributors

Adina Back has worked as a radio producer and labor educator and is currently the coordinator of public programs at the Jewish Museum in New York City.

Rachel Back is an Israeli poet.

Sara Back is coordinator for the New York City Department of Health, HIV serosurvey unit.

Toby Ticktin Back is a Jewish Studies educator and is the founder and director of Buffalo's Holocaust Resource Center. She is a wife, mother, and grandmother.

Bonnie Baron is a Licensed Clinical Social Worker who has experience working in family service agencies and in outpatient chemical dependency clinics.

Lawrence Baron is the Nasatir Professor of Modern Jewish History and Director of the Lipinsky Institute for Judaic Studies at San Diego State University. Both he and Bonnie have been active members of their local infertility support group.

Naomi Bromberg Bar-Yam is a social worker, childbirth educator, and needleworker. She creates life-cycle rituals, prayers, and *midrashim* to help women and their families celebrate passages and transitions in their lives. She lives with her husband and three children in Rehovot, Israel.

Cantor Judith Bender lives in the Los Angeles area and is associated with Temple Emanuel of Beverly Hills and Adat AriEl of North Hollywood. She has held the position of Cantor in Conservative congregations in California, New York, and Florida. Cantor Bender studied with Hazzan Lawrence Avery of New York, and is presently the student of Hazzan Nathan Lam of Los Angeles.

Tara Blau is an educator living in Albany.

Harry Brod teaches Gender Studies and Philosophy at Kenyon College in Ohio, where he lives with Maria Papacostaki and their children, Artemis and Alexi. He is the editor of *A Mensch Among Men: Explorations in Jewish Masculinity.*

Dina Dahbany-Miraglia, Ph.D., an independent scholar, is a linguistic anthropologist/performance artist who is based in New York. She has published articles on Yemenites and has lectured extensively on the Middle East, especially on women, and on Judeo Yemeni.

Dennis Danziger is a screenwriter and the author of *Daddy, The Diary of an Expectant Father.*

Rabbi Sue Levi Elwell is the Coordinator of the Los Angeles Jewish Feminist Center of the American Jewish Congress and serves as the rabbi of the Irvine Jewish Community.

Irene Fine, Ph.D., is Director of The Woman's Institute for

Continuing Jewish Education in San Diego. She is the author of *Educating The New Jewish Woman; Midlife, A Rite of Passage* and *The Wise Woman, A Celebration.*

Jerilyn Fisher, daughter of Arlene, daughter of Lillian, daughter of Sarah, daughter of Bluma, loves to celebrate birthdays. She has celebrated her daughter, Arielle's, birthday eight times and her son, Devan's, five times, rejoicing each year with her husband, Jules, and mother, Arlene, whose own mother, Lillian, gave birth to her on the same day as Arielle was born, two generations later. Jerilyn teaches English at the City University of New York's Hostos Community College in the Bronx.

Miriyam Glazer, Ph.D., is Associate Professor of Literature and Chair of the Department of English and Literature at the Lee College of the University of Judaism, Los Angeles. She is the author of numerous articles and the first collection in English of poetry by Israeli women, entitled *Burning Air and a Clear Mind: Contemporary Israeli Women Poets.*

Wendy Goulston, daughter of Jean, daughter of May, daughter of Bertha, all strong nurturing Australian Jewish women, teaches literature and writing at Empire State College. She celebrates and grows with her students, her colleagues and friends, as well as with her husband, Larry, and their two children, Tamara and Benjamin.

Rabbi Julie Greenberg directs the Jewish Renewal Life Center, a progressive yeshiva in Philadelphia offering a year of immersion in Jewish living and learning. She is the mother of Rosie and Raffi.

Nina Katz is a lexicographer and poet living in the Boston area.

Elizabeth Resnick Levine is a writer and editor with an M.A. in Jewish Studies from Hebrew Union College-Jewish Institute of Religion. She lives in San Diego with her husband, Andrew Resnick, son, Harry Akiva, and two charming dogs, Goniff and Kugel.

Rabbi Jane Litman is Director of Synagogue Affairs for the Western Region of the Reconstructionist Movement and Associate Rabbi of Congregation Tiferet Jacob. She has been organizing Jewish women's groups, teaching Jewish women's history, and writing feminist liturgy since 1977.

Maria Papacostaki teaches in the Humanities at Kenyon College in Ohio, where she lives with Harry Brod and their children, Artemis and Alexi.

Ellen Sandler is a film and television writer. She has taught writing at the University of Judaism and UCLA. She is the mother of two children, Jesse Max and Molly Bess.

Rabbi Sandy Eisenberg Sasso is the first woman to graduate from the Reconstructionist Rabbinical College in Philadelphia in 1974. She holds a B.A. and M.A. from Temple University and an honorary Doctorate of Humanities from DePauw University. Rabbi Sasso has written extensively on topics involving women, language, and ritual in religion. She served as President of the Reconstructionist Rabbinical Association from 1989 to 1991. She and her husband, Dennis C. Sasso, are the rabbis of Congregation Beth-El Zedeck in Indianapolis. They are parents of two children, David and Deborah.

Susan Saxe is the executive director of P'nai Or Religious Fellowship. Moon Smith and Susan Saxe met in 1983 in a Rosh Hodesh group in Philadelphia.

Amy Sheldon is married, the mother of two young girls, and is a writer and professor at the University of Minnesota.

Nancy Helman Shneiderman is a psychotherapist in private practice in Washington, D.C. She has two daughters and has been married for 18 years.

Hanna Tiferet Siegel is a Jewish spiritual teacher of the heart and hand. She lives in Hanover, New Hampshire, and dreams of living in a peaceful, loving community that celebrates the Divine Presence in everything.

Rachel Josefowitz Siegel is a sixty-five-year-old feminist psychotherapist, lecturer, and writer. She is co-editor of *Jewish Women in Therapy: Seen But Not Heard.* Her current professional interests focus on women over sixty, Jewish women, and counteracting mother-blaming.

Barbara Kochman Singer has a bachelor's degree in Religious Studies from the University of California, Santa Cruz, and has taken graduate courses in Jewish studies at Brandeis University and Hebrew Union College. She lives with her husband and three children in North Hollywood, California, where she is involved in Isha L'Isha, the woman's spirituality group at Temple Beth Hillel.

Moon Smith is a certified Nurse Midwife currently in a hospital-based practice.

Shoshana Zonderman is a feminist psychotherapist and Jewish educator who lives in Northampton, Massachusetts, with her husband, Rabbi Saul Perlmutter, and her children, Ariela Yonit and Noam Dov. She is a member of Havurat ha-Emek and of B'not Esh, a Jewish feminist collective.

Please Add Your Own Ceremony Here